Keeping
CHRISTMAS

CREATIVE
PUBLISHING
international

MINNETONKA, MINNESOTA

www.creativepub.com

President/CEO: Michael Eleftheriou
Vice President/Publisher: Linda Ball
Vice President/Retail Sales & Marketing: Kevin Haas

KEEPING CHRISTMAS
Created by: The Editors of
Creative Publishing international, Inc.

Executive Editor: Elaine Perry
Managing Editor: Yen Le
Senior Editor: Linda Neubauer
Art Director: Deborah Pierce
Cover Designer: Megan Noller
Project Stylist: Joanne Wawra
Prop Stylists: Christine Jahns, Joanne Wawra
Samplemakers: Arlene Dohrman, Sheila Duffy,
Teresa Henn, Mary Beth Kissling
Photo Stylists: Christine Jahns, John Rajtar,
Joanne Wawra
Photographers: Tate Carlson, Chuck Nields,
Andrea Rugg
Director of Production Services: Kim Gerber
Contributors: Apropolis, C.M. Offray and Son, Inc.,
June Tailor, Smith & Hawken, Walnut Hallow

ISBN 1-58923-049-3

Printed on American paper by:
R. R. Donnelly & Sons Co.
10 9 8 7 6 5 4 3 2 1

Library of Congress Cataloging-in-Publication Data

Keeping Christmas : preserving holiday memories & creating family
traditions.
    p. cm.
    ISBN 1-58923-049-3 (soft cover)
    1. Christmas decorations. 2. Handicraft. I. Creative Publishing
International.

TT900.C4 K43 2002
745.591'12--dc21

                                    2002017356

Creative Publishing international, Inc. offers
a variety of how-to books. For information write:
    Creative Publishing international, Inc.
    Subscriber Books
    5900 Green Oak Drive
    Minnetonka, MN 55343

Keeping
CHRISTMAS

Contents

Introduction 7

Preserving Christmas Memories 9

Matting & Framing Original Christmas Photos 11
Displaying Christmas Photos 14
Tinting of Black & White Photos 16
Photograph Ornaments 18
Shadow Box Ornaments 22
Photo Quilt 24
Silk Tie Christmas Decorations 28
Cookie Cutter & Recipe Ornament 32
Family Recipe Book 34
Handkerchief Angel 36
Crocheted Doily Ornament 37
Ornament Storage 38
Heirloom Christmas Tray 42

Decorating with Heirlooms 45

Toy Horses 46
Heirloom China in Centerpiece Displays 48
Music Themed Displays 49
Vintage Ornaments 50
Heritage Dolls 51
Copper Collection 52
Sleigh Bells & Garland 54
Wooden Firkens 56
Nostalgic Christmas Postcards 58
Christmas Memories Shadow Box 61

Creating Christmas Traditions 65

Christmas Memories Album 66
Add-a-Charm Christmas Stocking 70
Christmas Eve Pillowcase 72
Countdown Christmas Tree 74
Making Family Christmas Cards 76
Christmas Card Album 82
Autographed Christmas Tablecloth 84
Christmas Grow Chart 86
Santa Cookie Plate 88
Dear Santa Album 90
Pass-it-on Gift Box 94
Forcing Bulbs for Holiday Blooms 98
Sharing Heirloom Plants 100
Wildlife Gift Tree 102

Patterns 104

Index 111

Sources 112

Preserving
Christmas
Memories
9

Decorating
with
Heirlooms
45

Creating
Christmas
Traditions
65

Introduction

The word *keeping* is so fitting for the title of this book because it has a double meaning. In one sense, keeping Christmas means commemorating, celebrating, and honoring this most cherished holiday. In our spiritual and social gatherings with neighbors, family, and friends, we keep Christmas. In observing age-old traditions or starting new ones, we keep Christmas. Interpreted another way, keeping means saving, preserving, and caring for the special memories and traditions that are, for us and our families, the essence of Christmas. Unless we deliberately take precautions to safeguard the photographs and mementos that tell our family Christmas story and sustain our holiday heritage, they may be forgotten by our heirs.

Christmas, like no other time of year, is awash with memories from childhood. Classic Christmas movies and familiar music kindle longing glances back into eras when simpler living gave rise to more meaningful celebrations. Old Christmas photographs, vintage ornaments, heirloom toys, and even time-honored recipes are cherished for their ability to transport us back to those wonderful times. In this book, you will find many ways to incorporate these treasures into your holiday celebration, to enrich your family Christmas. You will also discover ways to organize and preserve your Christmas heirlooms, using archival quality techniques and materials to ensure that your treasures are enjoyed by future generations.

It is an interesting paradox that modern technology shares a space in our homes with old photographs and antique furniture. Love and admiration for simply crafted items, reminiscent of bygone days, coexist with our desire to master the mind-boggling complexity of high-tech home computer systems. Some of the projects in this book take advantage of computer capabilities to duplicate old Christmas photos, holiday correspondence, and children's artwork so they can be used creatively without compromising the integrity of the originals.

In addition to preserving Christmas memories, you will also find ideas and projects for creating new Christmas traditions in your family. Aside from the classic Christmas practices of various cultures and nationalities, these are intended to emphasize family bonds and instill in children of all ages an appreciation for their personal heritage. Included are a few activities and hand-crafted items intended for young children, whose enthusiasm and anticipation always heighten the Christmas spirit for those around them.

Keeping Christmas—commemorating and celebrating it—means different things to different families, and to the same families in different stages of life. Keeping Christmas—preserving the memories—is an ongoing process, entrusted from one generation to the next. Hopefully the ideas and projects presented in this book will help your family enrich and preserve its Christmas heritage.

Preserving Christmas Memories

Matting & Framing
Original Christmas Photos

Old Christmas photographs give us a window to Christmases past. They help us recall those special occasions and remember vividly the faces of old friends and relatives, even ancestors we never knew. In many ways, these old photographs help complete the puzzle of who we are, giving us access to our ancestral history. In the same way, the Christmas photographs you take today of your family and friends will provide a visual record and memory stimulus for generations to come. It is for this reason that extra care should be taken to preserve your Christmas photos.

Christmas photographs, old or new, can be matted and framed for a traditional look. Matting serves a dual purpose; it complements the photo aesthetically and keeps it from touching the glass. To make sure that these cherished images can be handed down from generation to generation, frame them using the techniques for conservation framing. With conservation framing, the materials and methods used help protect photographs from atmospheric acidity and sunlight and allow for expansion during high humidity.

To protect photographs from acids that cause yellowing and disintegration, use acid-free, lignin-free mat boards and mounting boards. For maximum protection, select conservation quality boards made from 100% cotton rag. Most precut mats are not archival quality, unless stated on the label. Those labeled "acid neutral" are less expensive and come in more colors than true conservation quality mats but offer less protection. Select metal frames whenever possible. Apply clear acrylic finish to any raw wood in a wooden frame to seal the acids in the wood. To best preserve the framed item, use UV-protective glass. While this glass is more expensive than standard glass, it provides protection from 95% of the sun's damaging ultraviolet rays.

Linen framer's tape is the preferred tape for mounting because it is acid free. Acid-neutral double-stick transfer tape, or adhesive transfer gum (ATG) tape, may be used to attach the paper dustcover to the back of the frame.

How to Bevel-cut a Mat

You will need:

- Acid-free mounting board
- Acid-free mat board and mat cutter, for mounting a picture with a mat
- 1" (2.5 cm) linen framer's tape, for hinge-mounting
- Acid-free, lignin-free adhesive photo corners
- Utility knife; cork-backed metal straightedge
- Cotton gloves

1 Subtract ⅛" (3 mm) from the dimensions of the frame opening to determine the size to cut the mat board; mark the wrong side of the mat board, making sure the corners are square. Using a utility knife and a straightedge, score repeatedly along the marked line until the board is cut through.

2 Carefully measure and mark the mat opening on the wrong side of the mat board. The opening should be at least ⅛" (3 mm) smaller than the photograph. Extend the lines almost to the edge of the board.

3 Place a scrap of mat board under the area to be cut. Using a straightedge, align the edge of the mat cutter with the marked line, placing the start-and-stop line (arrow) of the cutter even with the upper border line.

4 Push the blade into the mat. Cut on the marked line in one smooth pass; stop when the start-and-stop line meets the lower border line. Pull the blade out of the mat. Repeat to cut the remaining sides.

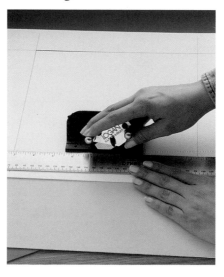

How to Mount a Photograph with a Mat

1 Bevel-cut the mat board (left). Cut the mounting board the same size as the mat. Place the photograph between the mat and mounting board. Wearing cotton gloves to protect the photo, gently ease the photo into position on the mounting board.

2 Remove the mat, keeping the photo in position. Secure the photo to the mounting board, using adhesive photo corners.

3 Fold a 3" (7.5 cm) strip of linen framer's tape in half, adhesive side out. Secure the underside of the strip to the mounting board about 1" (2.5 cm) from the end, with the folded edge of the strip aligned to the upper edge of the mounting board. Repeat at the opposite end.

4 Position the mat on the mounting board, aligning the edges; adhere the mat to the tape.

How to Assemble a Matted Photo in a Wooden Frame

You will need:

- Wooden picture frame and glass; clear acrylic finish for sealing raw wood of frame
- ¾" (2 cm) brads
- Framer's fitting tool or slip-joint pliers
- Brown craft paper
- Double-stick transfer tape, or ATG tape
- Two small screw eyes
- Self-adhesive rubber bumpers
- Small awl; braided picture wire; masking tape

1 Seal any raw wood of the frame, using clear acrylic finish; allow to dry. Clean both sides of the glass thoroughly, using glass cleaner and lint-free cloth.

2 Position the glass over the mounted photo and mat, with edges even. Place the frame over the glass. Slide your fingers under the mounting board, and turn the frame over.

3 Insert ¾" (2 cm) brads into the middle of each side of the frame, using a framer's fitting tool or a slip-joint pliers. If using a pliers, protect the outside edge of the frame with a strip of cardboard.

4 Recheck the face of the photo for lint or dust, remove the brads and clean the glass again, if necessary. Insert the brads along each side, 1" (2.5 cm) from the corners and at about 2" (5 cm) intervals.

5 Attach double-stick transfer tape to the frame back, about ⅛" (3 mm) from the outside edges; remove the paper covering. Cut the backing paper 2" (5 cm) larger than the frame.

6 Place the paper on the frame back, securing it to the center of each edge and stretching the paper taut. Working from the center out to each corner, stretch the paper and secure it to the frame. Crease the paper over the frame edge. Using a straightedge and a utility knife, trim the paper about ⅛" (3 mm) inside the creased line.

7 Mark the placement for screw eyes, about one-third down from the upper edge; secure screw eyes into the frame. Thread wire two or three times through one screw eye; twist the end. Repeat at the opposite side, allowing slack; wire is usually about 2" to 3" (5 to 7.5 cm) from the frame top when hung.

8 Cover the wire ends with masking tape. Secure rubber bumpers to the lower corners of the frame back.

Displaying Christmas Photos

*C*hristmas photos, whether old or new, can be displayed in many creative ways, adding interest to holiday décor and sparking conversation during Christmas gatherings. Photos can be reproduced with excellent clarity on modern color printers and home computer systems. With the added capabilities of changing photo sizes, cropping, and even changing color, it is possible for us to use and enjoy these precious images without causing harm to the originals.

Images, sandwiched between layers of glass, seemingly float in midair. They can be accented with precut paper frames, available at scrapbooking stores. Similarly, a series of Santa visit photos, taken over the years, can be used to create a set of holiday coasters.

How to Mount Photos in Glass

You will need:

- Two pieces of ⅛" (3 mm) glass, cut 2" (5 cm) larger than the photo
- Die-cut paper frame
- Christmas photo; copy machine or computer with scanner and printer
- Small binder clips
- ⅜" (1 cm) foil tape

1 Clean both surfaces of both pieces of glass with glass cleaner and lint-free cloth or paper towel. Copy the photo, cropping and sizing it to fit inside the paper frame. Write names and date on the back of the image, if desired. Position the image in the center of one glass; place the frame over it. Cover with the other glass.

2 Hold the pieces firmly together, using small binder clips. Peel back a little of the paper backing from the strip of foil tape. Beginning at the lower edge, apply the foil tape to the glass edges, centering the tape so equal amounts will wrap to the front and back. Continue around the glass, removing binder clips as you go. Overlap the tape slightly at the end; cut the tape.

3 Cut the tape up to the glass at each corner on both sides. Fold the tape to the front and back, smoothing it in place; lap one side over the other at each corner.

4 Smooth all sides of the foil tape firmly, using the handle of a wooden spoon or a wooden craft stick to ease out any bubbles.

How to Make Photo Coasters

You will need:

- ⅛" (3 mm) plexiglass cut into 3½" (9 cm) squares; two per coaster
- Christmas photos; copy machine or computer with scanner and printer
- Narrow masking tape
- ⅜" (1 cm) foil tape
- Self-adhesive felt circles

1 Clean both surfaces of both pieces of plexiglass with glass cleaner and lint-free cloth or paper towel. Copy the photos, cropping and sizing them to 3" (7.5 cm) squares. Write names and dates on the backs of the images, if desired. Position an image in the center of one plexiglass square. Cover with the other glass.

2 Finish the coasters, following steps 2 to 4 above. Adhere four felt circles to the back side of each coaster, over the photo corners.

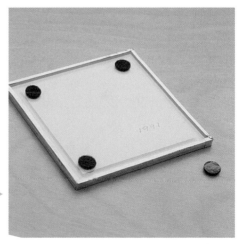

Tinting of Black & White Photos

Black and white photographs, lightly tinted in pastel shades, offer a mystical window to the past. In a simpler time, before color photography, hand-coloring of black and white photos gave them an animation that couldn't be achieved otherwise. It was a meticulous, time-consuming process reserved for artists. Today you can create a similar look for vintage or contemporary photographs, with far less fuss.

There are several methods and products available for hand-tinting black and white photographs. Some methods are more complex and expensive than others, requiring the use of several products, including photo conditioners, tinting oils, and finishing sprays. However, Zig® Photo Twin™ pens, are much easier to use and produce excellent results without much practice. The pens, which have both small and large brush tips, are photo safe and acid free. They come in sets of six color wands, either in bright tones for vibrant color or in pastel shades for a more subtle effect. A softener pen is also available for blending colors or creating very subtle shades.

Hand-tinting is most successful on close-up shots and simple subjects. The pens are not effective over dark areas, so look for photos in which the subjects are wearing light-colored clothing or accessories or have light-colored skin and hair. Never use an original photo unless you have its negative. Instead, have copies made at a photo shop, or scan and print the photos yourself, preferably on matte photo paper. Even colored photos can be printed in black and white for hand-tinting.

Practice using the pens to become familiar with the colors and the process. Use the small brush tip for the lightest application of color and in smaller areas. For a single swash of color, hold the large brush tip on its side and make one quick sweep across the area. Avoid coloring in complete areas of one color. Rather, apply hints of color, such as a touch of "blush" to create rosy cheeks or soft golden highlight streaks in the hair. Apply short, quick strokes with the softener pen while the color is still wet to blend color areas together or to soften harsh outlines.

No finishing spray is necessary when photos have been tinted with Photo Twin pens. The colors dry to the touch fairly quickly, but the finished photos should be allowed to air-dry for a day or so before storing them in sheet protectors or mounting them behind glass.

Matte-finish photos and copies made on acid-free, lignin-free heavy paper can also be tinted with decorating chalks. Simply apply the color with small cosmetic applicators and spray with fixative to complete the project.

Photograph Ornaments

Heirloom photographs of your ancestors or contemporary family photographs taken at Christmas are easily turned into precious Christmas ornaments.

Various objects can be used as lightweight frames for the photos, with ribbons or cords tied on for hanging and holiday trims and findings added for festivity. It may be as simple as inserting the photo into a miniature frame and attaching a ribbon hanger. Keep in mind that the photograph is the main attraction; all other elements used for the ornament should enhance the photo.

Begin by scanning and copying the photographs, so the originals can be stored for safekeeping. Make sure the focal point of the photo will be centered on the ornament. When working with a color photo,

select a single color for the frame that will accent the face in the photo. Frame a black and white glossy photo with more colorful background, if you desire, keeping any designs small to avoid drawing the eye away from the photo. To achieve a vintage look, print the photos in sepia tones and use subdued velvets or antique laces as framing materials. Print out black and white photos on matte photo paper and tint them lightly (page 16) for an old-fashioned effect. Frame them in light pastel colors. If you don't have access to a scanner and printer, take your photos or negatives to a print shop or photo shop to have them copied.

How to Make a Lace Ornament

You will need:

- ♦ Copied photograph
- ♦ Lace coaster
- ♦ Spray starch; iron
- ♦ Heavyweight paper
- ♦ Circle cutter
- ♦ Spray adhesive
- ♦ Fabric glue
- ♦ Narrow ribbon

1 Copy the photo; glue it to heavyweight paper, using spray adhesive. Measure the center diameter of the coaster, or the area you wish to cover. Cut out the photo in a circle with this diameter, using a circle cutter for accuracy. Cut a second circle of paper.

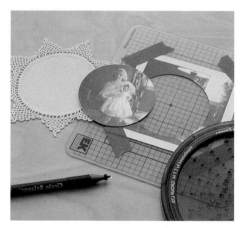

2 Stiffen the coaster, if necessary, using spray starch. Glue the photo circle to the front of the coaster, using fabric glue. Write a short description of the photo on the paper circle; glue it to the back of the ornament.

3 Cut a 14" (35.5 cm) length of ribbon; slip it through a hole in the outer edge of the coaster top, and tie the ends together.

How to Make a Photo Transfer Quilted Diamond Ornament

You will need:

- ♦ Copied photograph
- ♦ June Tailor Quick Fuse™ Inkjet Fabric Sheets
- ♦ Cotton velveteen fabric or other fancy fabric
- ♦ Machine embroidery thread
- ♦ Sewing machine
- ♦ Low-loft batting
- ♦ Narrow decorative trim
- ♦ Fabric glue
- ♦ Narrow ribbon or cord

1 Trace and cut out the pattern on page 104. Scan and print the photograph on inkjet fabric sheet, sizing it to fit the pattern. Cut photo print into an oval, using the pattern. Cut two pieces of fabric and a piece of batting 1/2" (1.3 cm) larger than the pattern.

2 Trace the diamond pattern on the wrong side of one of the fabric pieces. Cut a 1 1/2" (3.8 cm) vertical slit in the center of the marked piece. Place the pieces right sides together; pin to the batting, with the marked surface facing up. Stitch around the marked line.

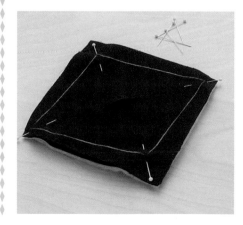

3 Trim excess fabric away to within 1/4" (6 mm) of stitching. Turn the diamond right side out through the slit. Press lightly.

4 Fuse the photo print in place over the slit, following the manufacturer's directions.

5 Stitch around the outer edge of the photo print. Adhere narrow decorative trim around the outer edge, covering the stitches, using fabric glue. Make a ribbon loop, and hand-stitch it to the ornament top.

How to Decoupage a Papier-Mâché Ornament

You will need:

- Copied photograph
- Papier-mâché ornament with flat surface
- Acrylic craft paint
- Card stock
- Scissors with scallop blades
- Decoupage medium
- Foam applicator
- Narrow decorative trim
- Narrow ribbon or cord

1 Paint the ornament; allow to dry. Scan and print the photo, sizing it to fit the flat surface.

2 Cut a card stock shape, ¼" (6 mm) smaller than the flat area, using a scissors with scallop blades. Cut the photo to fit just inside the scallop edge; adhere to the card stock, using decoupage medium. Allow to dry. Adhere mounted photo to ornament, using decoupage medium.

3 Cut a card stock shape to fit the ornament back; write a short description of the photo, and adhere it to the ornament back. Apply several thin coats of the decoupage medium over the entire surface of the shape, allowing it to dry completely between coats.

4 Glue narrow decorative trim around the outside of the ornament. Make a loop for hanging.

How to Make a Snowflake Frame Ornament

You will need:

- Copied photograph
- White heavy card stock
- Craft knife and cutting mat
- Round hole paper punches in two sizes
- Spray adhesive; craft glue
- Blue marker
- Fine white glitter
- Narrow ribbon

1 Trace the snowflake pattern (page 105); cut out. Trace the pattern twice on heavy card stock. Cut out the snowflakes, using a craft knife and cutting mat. Cut the frame opening out of the center of one snowflake; save the cutout. Trace the opening onto the other snowflake.

2 Copy the photograph; cut it in the shape shown on the pattern. Apply spray adhesive to the frame back; adhere the photo to the center over the marked lines. Secure the frame front to the back. Draw accent lines and dots on the frame front, using a blue marker.

3 Punch holes in the snowflake arms, using hole punches in two sizes. Insert the cutout over the photo; spray snowflake front with adhesive. Sprinkle with glitter, shake off excess, and allow to dry. Repeat on snowflake back.

4 Cut a 14" (35.5 cm) length of ribbon; slip it through the top hole, and tie the ends together.

Shadow Box Ornaments

Personal treasures from the past are showcased in unique shadow box ornaments. Made from small lidded boxes, each ornament also carries a written history of its precious cache and a photograph of the original owner. Heirlooms from your ancestors, such as pocket watches, brooches, cameos, class rings, or military medals, are items that can be featured in shadow box ornaments. As a commemorative ornament for a birth in the family, the ornament might house a small rattle, a pair of booties, or a pacifier. An ornament for newlyweds could feature a dried boutonniere, a garter, or a trinket from the wedding cake.

How to Make a Shadow Box Ornament

You will need:

- Cardboard, wood, or papier-mâché box with lid
- Acrylic craft paints or stain
- Suede paper
- Craft glue
- Keepsake item
- Photograph of owner
- Paper for writing description
- Decoupage medium
- Narrow ribbon
- Awl or drill; darning needle
- Preserved greens or berries or other trimmings as desired

1 Paint all surfaces of the box and lid; allow to dry. Cut a piece of suede paper ¼" (6 mm) wider than the inside box depth and ¼" (6 mm) longer than the inside circumference. Cut ¼" (6 mm) clips on one long edge of the strip, spacing them ¼" (6 mm) apart. Apply craft glue to the wrong side, and secure to the inside of the box, aligning the cut edge to the box top and lapping the clipped edge onto the box bottom.

2 Cut a piece of suede paper to fit the inside box bottom. Apply glue to the wrong side, and adhere to the box bottom, covering the clipped edge from step 1.

3 Make a copy of the photo, so the original can be stored for safekeeping. Determine the angle at which you want the shadow box to hang on its side. Cut the photo to the shape of the box top, cutting it slightly smaller than marked, and centering the face. Adhere the photo to the box top.

4 Trace the box bottom on a sheet of paper. Within the shape, write a brief note about the featured keepsake, noting to whom it belonged and any significant dates; keep in mind the angle at which the box will hang. Cut out the note, cutting it slightly smaller than marked, and adhere it to the outside box bottom. Apply decoupage medium.

5 Apply any other flat decorations or painted designs to the outside of the box as desired. Apply several thin coats of decoupage medium to the outer surfaces of the box and lid, allowing them to dry between coats.

6 Poke or drill a small hole in the center of the box side that will be at the top when the box is hung. Secure the keepsake to the center of a long ribbon. Thread both ends of the ribbon onto a darning needle and through the hole from the inside. Tie the tails into a bow on the outside so the keepsake is suspended inside the box.

7 Tie the bow loops again to secure; tie the tail ends together, forming a loop for hanging. Secure any other embellishments to the ornament top as desired. To store the ornament, simply cover with the photo lid. Remove the lid and place it on the box bottom when hanging the ornament.

Photo Quilt

Favorite Christmas photos can be printed on fabric and showcased in a delightfully festive quilted wall hanging. Nine star quilt blocks make up this 40" (102 cm) square quilt, with a special Christmas photo at the center of each star.

Professional services are available for transferring your photographs to fabric. There are also several products for transferring a photograph to fabric using your home computer and scanner. All methods allow you to preserve your original photos. In the method shown here, fabric is treated with a special product, Bubble Jet Set 2000®, that allows it to accept and hold inkjet printer inks. The treated fabric is mounted to freezer paper so that it can be fed through the printer. The photo is actually printed on the fabric, and the paper easily peels away after printing. Because the fabric retains its original weight and hand, this method is highly favored among quilters and fabric artists.

How to Transfer Photos to Fabric

1 Wash and dry fabric for photo printing to shrink it and remove any sizing. Do not use fabric softener. Cut fabric into 9½" × 12" (24.3 × 30.5 cm) pieces. Place one piece in the bottom of a large plastic box; saturate with Bubble Jet Set 2000. Repeat with each piece until all fabric pieces are stacked and saturated with the solution. Allow to soak for five minutes.

2 Cover a large surface with plastic and old towels. Remove fabric pieces from solution; squeeze out excess solution. Lay pieces out on surface and allow to dry.

3 Place fabric pieces over the shiny side of freezer paper; press with dry iron until pieces bond to the paper and are free of bubbles. Using a rotary cutter and mat, trim the pieces to 8½" × 11" (21.8 × 28 cm).

4 Scan the photos. Reduce or enlarge them as desired, allowing for 4" (10 cm) square usable size. Under advanced print options, select the finest print quality, glossy photo paper, and vivid color. Print the photo first on plain paper to check quality. Adjust settings as necessary for remaining photos. Print two photos on each prepared fabric sheet, running the treated fabric through your inkjet printer.

5 Allow the printed fabric to sit for 30 minutes. Peel off the freezer paper. Wash printed pieces in wash machine with Bubble Jet Rinse or mild detergent and a large amount of water to remove any unreacted inks. Check occasionally to make sure prints are not folded or twisted. Machine dry along with an old towel.

You will need:

- 1 yd. (0.92 m) white or off-white, 100% cotton or silk fabric for the photo prints
- 5/8 yd. (0.6 m) each of two different small Christmas print fabrics for star points, outer border, and binding
- 3/4 yd. (0.7 m) light-colored fabric for star background

- 5/8 yd. (0.6 m) fabric for sashing and inner border
- 1 1/2 yd. (1.4 m) backing fabric
- 45" (115 cm) square of batting
- Bubble Jet Set 2000 solution
- Flat plastic box
- Freezer paper
- Iron

- Rotary cutter and mat; quilter's ruler
- Computer, scanner, and inkjet color printer
- Bubble Jet Rinse or mild detergent
- UV fabric protectant
- Lath for hanging, 1/2" (1.3 cm) shorter than finished quilt width

How to Make a Christmas Photo Quilt

1 Print nine different Christmas photos on fabric (page 24), allowing at least 1" (2.5 cm) space between them. Cut prints into 4½" (11.5 cm) squares, for star centers.

2 Cut 20 2⅞" (7.2 cm) squares for star points from one print fabric; cut 16 squares from other print. Cut squares in half diagonally.

3 Cut 36 2⅞" (7.2 cm) squares for star background; cut in half diagonally. Also cut 36 2½" (6.5 cm) squares of background fabric.

4 Cut eight 2½" (6.5 cm) strips on crosswise grain of fabric for sashing and inner border. For outer border, cut four 3½" (9 cm) strips on crosswise grain of fabric. For binding, cut four 3" (7.5 cm) strips on crosswise grain of fabric.

5 Place one background triangle on one star point triangle, right sides together. Stitch along the bias edge, using ¼" (6 mm) seam allowance. Repeat for all 72 sets, chainstitching pairs continuously.

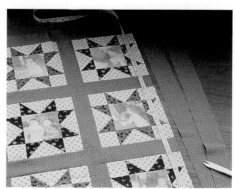

6 Clip pairs apart. Press seams toward print; avoid stretching the bias. Align two pairs along the background sides, right sides together; stitch. Repeat for all 36 sets, chainstitching units.

7 Clip units apart. Press seams to one side. Trim off the points at the two corners and center of opposite side of each unit. Stitch a background square to each end of half the units; press the seam allowances toward the squares.

8 Stitch a short unit to the top and bottom of each photo square, aligning the print edges to the square; press seam allowances toward the photo. Stitch longer units to the sides of each photo square, completing the blocks; press seam allowances toward the center.

9 Measure all sides of several quilt blocks to determine the shortest measurement; cut six sashing strips to this length. Stitch strips between blocks, right sides together, to form three rows; do not stitch strips to row ends. Press seams toward the sashing.

10 Measure the length of rows to determine the shortest measurement. Cut sashing strips to this length. Mark centers of strips and rows. Stitch strips between rows, right sides together, matching marks; ease in fullness. Press seams toward sashing.

11 Measure the top and bottom of quilt. Cut two inner border strips, with the length equal to the shorter measurement. Pin strip to upper edge of quilt top, right sides together, at center and at ends; pin along length, easing in any fullness. Stitch; press seams toward inner border. Repeat at lower edge.

12 Measure quilt sides, including inner border. Cut two inner border strips as in step 11. Pin and stitch to quilt sides as in step 11.

13 Repeat steps 11 and 12 for outer border. Cut fabric square for quilt backing about 4" (10 cm) larger than quilt top. Mark centers of all sides of backing, batting, and quilt top with safety pins. Tape the backing to the work surface, wrong side up; stretch fabric slightly.

14 Place batting over backing, matching marks on all sides; smooth, but do not stretch, working from center out to sides. Place quilt top, right side up, over batting, matching marks on all sides; smooth, but do not stretch, working from center out to sides.

15 Baste layers together with safety pins, working from the center out in each quadrant. Space safety pins about 6" (15 cm) apart, avoiding seams.

16 Beginning in center, quilt around each photo by stitching in the ditch. Then stitch around each star block. Stitch in the ditch of the seam between the inner and outer borders.

17 Measure one side of quilt; cut binding this length plus 2" (5 cm). Mark binding 1" (2.5 cm) from each end; divide section between marks in quarters, and mark. Divide side of quilt in quarters; mark.

18 Fold binding in half lengthwise, wrong sides together. Place binding on quilt top, matching raw edges and marks; binding extends 1" (2.5 cm) beyond quilt top at each end. Stitch 1/4" (6 mm) from raw edge of binding. Cut excess batting and backing to 1/2" (1.3 cm) from stitching line.

19 Wrap binding around edge of quilt, covering stitching line on back of quilt; pin. Stitch in the ditch on right side of quilt, catching binding on the back of the quilt.

20 Repeat steps 17 to 19 for opposite side of quilt. Trim binding ends even with edges of quilt top. Repeat steps 17 to 18 for remaining two sides. Trim binding ends to extend 1/2" (1.3 cm) beyond finished edges of quilt.

21 Fold the binding out along the stitching line. Fold binding end over finished edge; press in place. Wrap binding around edge and stitch in the ditch as in step 19. Slipstitch end by hand.

22 Cut washed, unbleached muslin strip, 10" (25.5 cm) wide by the width of quilt. Turn under and stitch double 1/2" (1.3 cm) hems at short ends. Stitch long edges of strip, right sides together, using 1/2" (1.3 cm) seam; press seam allowances open. Turn sleeve right side out; press flat, centering seam along the back.

23 Pin sleeve to back of quilt, close to edges. Blindstitch sleeve to quilt along top and bottom edges; stitch through backing and batting. To protect photo quilt from fading, spray with UV fabric protectant; follow manufacturer's directions. Insert a sealed wooden lath through the sleeve. Nail lath ends to the wall to hang the quilt.

Silk Tie Decorations

*O*ld silk ties, the colorful barometers of masculine fashion, also whipser the personal stories of the important men in our lives who wore them. With their kaleidoscope of distinctive patterns, they give us mental snapshots of special occasions and daily routines from the past.

Vintage fabrics from Dad's discarded neckties can be used to create sentimental decorations, like these patchwork hearts and stars, stuffed balls and teardrops, and circle chains. Though the ties may be worn, outdated, or stained, the fabrics often have exquisite designs and vibrant colors. Strips of the fancy bias fabrics can be used instead of ribbons for tying small packages. You may decide to use tie fabric to line the inside of an ornament storage box (page 38) or a shadow box ornament (page 22). If you have enough ties in the right colors, you could use them to make a memory quilt like the one on page 24.

Cutting the ties apart certainly destroys their integrity as fashion accessories. But their contribution of color, texture, and pattern to the finished project justifies the cutting and allows you to admire and remember the fabrics. (You have to crack a few eggs to make an omelette.) Begin by carefully taking the ties apart, using a seam ripper. Discard the interfacing, and hand-wash the ties in cold water with a mild detergent. After line-drying, press the creases out of the remaining tie fabric, taking care not to distort the fabric grain.

How to Make Patchwork Ornaments

You will need:

- Tie fabrics
- Lightweight fusible knit interfacing
- Paper
- Sewing machine; needle and thread
- Narrow silk ribbon; chenille needle
- Old buttons

1 Fuse interfacing to the wrong side of the tie fabrics, for strength and ease in handling. Trace the heart or star ornament pattern on page 106 or 107 onto paper; allow a 1" (2.5 cm) margin around the outside. Repeat for the back. For the heart, cut eight 4" (10 cm) squares of four different tie fabrics (two of each) for the sections of the pattern. Cut two 3" (7.5 cm) squares and three 3" × 5" (7.5 × 12.7 cm) pieces of different fabrics for the star.

2 Center and pin the wrong side of the fabric for section 1 to the back of the pattern; hold the pattern up to the light to help position the fabric so its edges extend at least 1/4" (6 mm) beyond section 1 design lines.

3 Place section 2 fabric over first piece, right sides together, aligning raw edges between sections 1 and 2. Pin along the shared design line; fold out second fabric and hold pattern up to the light to confirm that the fabric extends at least 1/4" (6 mm) beyond section 2 design lines. Adjust position of second fabric, if necessary.

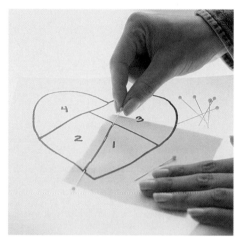

4 Unfold the second fabric. Using a short stitch length, stitch, paper side up, along the shared design line, extending the stitching a couple stitches beyond the line at both ends. Trim seam allowances to 1/4" (6 mm). Fold the second fabric away from the first; pin.

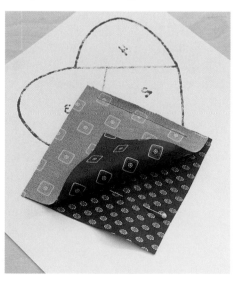

5 Repeat steps 3 and 4 for each consecutive section. Stitch around the entire ornament, just outside the design line. Trim the excess fabric 1/4" (6 mm) beyond the outer lines. Remove the paper.

6 Repeat steps 2 to 5 for the ornament back. Pin the front and back, right sides together. Stitch 1/4" (6 mm) from the edge, leaving a 2" (5 cm) opening along one flat side for turning.

7 Turn the ornament right side out through the opening. Stuff the ornament lightly with polyester fiberfill. Stitch the opening closed. Hand-stitch old buttons along top arches of the heart or on the star points and center.

8 Cut an 18" (46 cm) length of narrow silk ribbon; fold in half and tie a knot halfway between the fold and the ends. Thread the loop onto a chenille needle; draw the hanger through the ornament at the center top. Tie the tails into a bow.

How to Make Fabric Ball Ornaments

You will need:

- Tie fabrics
- Lightweight fusible knit interfacing
- Sewing machine; needle and thread
- Polyester fiberfill
- Fabric glue
- Narrow silk ribbon; chenille needle

1 Trace the desired pattern on page 106 onto paper. Fuse lightweight interfacing to the wrong side of four different tie fabrics. Cut a piece from each fabric, using the pattern. Transfer the dot to the wrong side of each piece.

2 Pin two pieces right sides together. Stitch from the short straight ends to the dot, 1/4" (6 mm) from the raw edges, using a short stitch length; backstitch at the dot.

3 Stitch third and fourth pieces to the unit, as in step 2. Stitch remaining seam, forming a closed shape.

4 Turn the ornament right side out through the opening. Stuff the ornament firmly with polyester fiberfill, using the eraser end of a pencil.

5 Gather the upper edge of the ornament 1/8" (3 mm) from the raw edge, using hand running stitches. Pull the gathering stitches tight, turning the raw edge to the inside. Knot securely.

6 Attach a hanger and bow, as in step 8, opposite. Thread two 9" (23 cm) lengths of silk ribbon onto the needle. Take a small stitch in the center bottom; draw the ribbons halfway through. Tie all tails together in an overhand knot tight against the bottom of the ornament, allowing the tails to hang free.

How to Make Fabric Circle Chains

You will need:

- Tie fabrics
- Fusible web
- Fabric glue
- Small spring-style clothespins
- Old buttons, optional

1 Fuse two tie fabrics wrong sides together. Cut 1" × 6" (2.5 × 15 cm) strips, running lengthwise on the fabrics. Because of the way ties are constructed, the strips will be bias.

2 Form a strip into a circle, overlapping the ends 1/4" (6 mm); secure with fabric glue. Clamp with small clothespin. Repeat with the next strip, using the reverse side out and linking it into the first circle. Repeat to the desired length. Remove clothespins. Stitch old buttons to the circles, if desired.

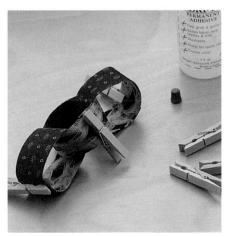

Cookie Cutter & Recipe Ornament

Old cookie cutters have long, sentimental stories to tell, especially if they are accompanied by handwritten cookie recipes. Both elements are combined in this wistful ornament. If you look closely, you can still see Grandmother's buttery fingerprints on the recipe card!

You will need:

- ♦ Well-used cookie cutter
- ♦ Handwritten cookie recipe
- ♦ Heavy, reversible decorative paper
- ♦ Narrow ribbon
- ♦ Darning needle   ♦ Tape
- ♦ Photo corners   ♦ Hole punch

1 Cut a rectangle of heavy decorative paper 1" (2.5 cm) larger than the recipe card or the cookie cutter, whichever is larger. Center the cookie cutter on one side of the paper. Thread a darning needle with narrow ribbon. Following one of the methods shown, lace and tie the cookie cutter to the paper.

How to Make a Cookie Cutter Ornament

2 Place photo corners on the corners of the recipe card. Secure the card to the opposite side of the ornament, covering the stitch holes.

3 Punch a hole in the top center of the ornament; tie a length of ribbon for hanging.

Cookie Cutter Tree

Gathering friends or family for a Christmas cookie baking day or a cookie exchange party is a popular holiday activity. Satisfying the old adage, "Many hands make light work," it also affords everyone a relaxing, creative escape from the frenzy. A miniature tree decorated with vintage cookie cutters is a tailor-made centerpiece for such a gathering. Swaddled around the base of the tree is an embroidered Christmas apron, once worn yearly for the same event in a previous generation.

Family Recipe Book

Favorite family recipes, passed down through generations of cooks, add so much to the culinary delights of the Christmas season. Spicy aromas wafting from the Christmas kitchen have the power to conjure up happy holiday memories from our childhood. If you are lucky enough to come from a family of pot luck lovers, perhaps you associate certain holiday foods with the individual relatives who usually prepare them.

As a gift for other family members and a keepsake for yourself, gather all those favorite recipes together in an album of family Christmas recipes. Ask family members from all the branches of your family tree to send you their specialty recipes, preferably written in their own handwriting, along with a snapshot of themselves, if you don't have one. You can always make a copy and return the original. Include journal entries for each of the recipes, recalling holiday meals shared together or enjoyable days of Christmas cookie baking. Be sure to add short biographies about each person. Scan and copy the recipes, photos, and journal entries, so that you can make an album as a gift for everyone who participates.

For our recipe book, we selected a red, cloth covered, album with removable, plastic-protected pages. Because we intend to actually use the recipe book often, we decorated the covers with easy-to-clean laminated fabric. The spine of this album is expandable and removable, and, because it matches our laminated fabric, we chose to leave it unadorned.

How to Make a Family Recipe Book

You will need:

- Cloth-covered, expandable album
- Laminated fabric
- Thin cardboard
- Rickrack
- Self-adhesive letters
- Adhesive

1 Cut fabric 1" (2.5 cm) larger than the front cover. Glue rickrack strips about 1½" (3.8 cm) from upper and lower edges. Turn under and glue ½" (1.3 cm) on the spine edge.

2 Glue the fabric to the cover, wrapping it to the inside. Clip and overlap the fabric at the corners to reduce bulk.

3 Repeat steps 1 and 2 for the back cover. Finish the inside covers, following steps 6 to 8 on page 93.

4 Affix self-adhesive title letters to the front cover.

Handkerchief Angel

Great grandmother's dainty handkerchiefs, neatly folded and tucked away in a drawer, are cherished but rarely admired. As a precious remembrance of the dear lady and a fitting complement to your Christmas decor, this tree topper angel wears a splendid gown, fashioned from three of those beloved, demure hankies. If you are unable to find three suitable handkerchiefs, substitute two purchased handkerchiefs for the back and sleeves of the gown.

You will need:

- ◆ Three heirloom handkerchiefs
- ◆ Plastic craft cone, 9" (23 cm) tall
- ◆ 3¼" (8.2 cm) porcelain doll head and shoulders with hands
- ◆ White chenille stem
- ◆ Angel wings
- ◆ Hand needle and thread
- ◆ Satin ribbon
- ◆ Craft ring or ring of small pearls for halo
- ◆ Hot glue gun

How to Make a Handkerchief Angel

1 Bend back the ends of a white chenille stem so it measures 9" (23 cm). Secure porcelain hands to ends, using hot glue. Fold one handkerchief into thirds, enclosing the chenille stem; tie at the center with thread, forming sleeves.

2 Center sleeves over the cone, with open edges facing down; make sure hands are on the correct sides. Insert cone up into porcelain head, keeping sleeves to the sides. Secure cone to head with dots of hot glue under front and back lower edges, avoiding fabric.

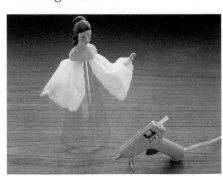

3 Beginning in the center of the gown back handkerchief, stitch ¼" (6 mm) running stitches just below the hem. Lap the front handkerchief over the back one ½" (1.3 cm) at the edges and continue stitching, joining them into a circle. Pull up on the ends, gathering the handkerchiefs around the shoulders; knot securely in the back.

4 Tie a ribbon around the angel, just under the shoulders and sleeves; tie a bow in the back. Adjust the gown gathers evenly, lapping the gown front over the back under the sleeves. Hand-tack the wings to the angel back.

5 Secure a craft ring or ring of small pearls to the head, using a dot of hot glue at the back. Open out the ends of the sleeves; pose the hands as desired.

Crocheted Doily Ornament

*R*ound lacy doilies that once graced tabletops or dressers in Grandmother's house find new life as featured attractions on your Christmas tree. These easy-to-make ornaments showcase treasured handiwork as well as an heirloom button or a memorable piece of jewelry.

How to Make a Doily Ornament

1 Insert the cord into the ornament hanger, and tie the ends. Wrap the doily around the ball, with the center of the doily at the bottom of the ball. Tie ribbon around the doily at the top of the ball; knot.

2 Run ribbon ends through the shank of an heirloom button; tie ribbon into a bow. Or tie a bow and pin a brooch over it.

You will need:

- ◆ 12" (30.5 cm) round crocheted doily
- ◆ 3" or 3½" (7.5 or 9 cm) colored ball ornament
- ◆ 9" (23 cm) length of narrow cord or ribbon for hanging ornament
- ◆ 22" (56 cm) narrow ribbon
- ◆ Heirloom button or brooch

Ornament Storage

Vintage Christmas tree ornaments, perhaps passed down to you from your great grandparents, are not just collector's items. They carry with them your family history and give you the privilege of carrying on a family tradition. Whether made of blown glass, carved wood, or intricately cut paper, their delicate nature calls for special care and handling. Likewise, special ornaments that you make, buy, or receive from from loved ones require proper storage, so that generations from now, your descendants can admire them and tell their stories.

For safekeeping, wrap your special ornaments in acid-free tissue paper and store them in individual decorated boxes or in photo storage boxes with cardboard dividers. Rest delicate ornaments in a bed of shredded paper or polyester fiberfill. Decorate the individual boxes with fancy papers and trims, signifying their importance. Include a brief description of the ornament, its origin, and family significance.

Collectible ornaments are often more valuable if they still have their original boxes. However, years of opening and closing those boxes could cause excessive wear and tear. It may be wise to collapse and store the boxes separately to retain their value.

As an added precaution in protecting your ornament collection, keep a record in a small journal. Include pictures and information about the ornaments, the dates they were received, and from whom. In the event that the journal should ever become separated from the ornament collection, or the ornaments become separated from their boxes, your heirs will be better able to identify them.

Various adhesives can be used to attach the decorative papers to the boxes and to the journal. Diluted craft glue or premixed wallpaper paste can be applied, using a sponge applicator. Spray adhesive can also be used. Thick craft glue and clear fabric glue are useful for attaching braids and trims. Test the adhesive first to be sure it won't soak through and discolor the paper or trim.

How to Decorate an Ornament Storage Box

You will need:

- Cardboard or papier-mâché box with lid, large enough to hold the ornament and packing material
- Decorative papers
- Decorative trims, ribbons, tassels, buttons, or charms as desired
- Adhesives; sponge applicator

1 Separate the lid from the box. Cut a rectangle of paper with the width and length equal to twice the box height plus the box bottom plus 2" (5 cm). Place the box in the center; lightly trace around the bottom.

2 Lay the box on its side, keeping the bottom aligned to the traced line; trace the side, extending to the outer edge of the rectangle. Repeat for each side. On two opposing sides, draw ¼" (6 mm) tabs as shown. Cut out.

3 Apply adhesive to the box or paper. Cover the box, beginning with the bottom. Secure the tabbed sides first, wrapping the tabs onto the adjacent sides. Secure the remaining sides. Fold the upper extensions down inside the box.

4 Cut a rectangle of paper to cover the lid, with the width and length equal to the lid measurement plus four times the lid height. Trace the lid in the center of the rectangle. Repeat steps 2 to 3 for the box lid.

5 Secure ribbons, braided trims, button, tassels, or other embellishments as desired. Print a brief description and history of the ornament on a card; secure to the inside of the lid.

How to Make Dividers for a Storage Box

You will need:

- Acid-free mat board
- Utility knife and cutting board
- Straightedge

1 Cut one piece of mat board the inside length and height of the box; cut two pieces the width and height of the box.

2 Cut a slit in the center of each short piece slightly longer than half the width; the slit width should equal the thickness of the mat board. Divide the long piece into thirds. Cut slits at the marks, slightly longer than half the width.

3 Slide the boards together at the slits; insert into the box. Create a label for the box, identifying the six ornaments stored inside.

How to Embellish an Ornament Journal

You will need:

- Bound book-style journal
- Decorative paper to coordinate with the original book cover
- Spray adhesive, glue stick, diluted craft glue, or premixed wallpaper paste
- ⅝" (15 mm) ribbon
- Card stock in two colors to coordinate with the paper
- Bone folder or wooden craft stick
- Corner slot punch

1 Cut a rectangle of paper 1" (2.5 cm) narrower and 1" (2.5 cm) longer than the book cover. Apply adhesive to the wrong side of the paper. Adhere paper to book front cover, 1½" (3.8 cm) from the spine; top, bottom, and front edges will extend ½" (1.3 cm). Trim the corners as shown, ⅛" (3 mm) from the corners.

2 Wrap top and bottom extensions to the inside; wrap front extension to the inside. Smooth all surfaces, using a bone folder tool or a wooden craft stick.

3 Repeat steps 1 and 2 for back cover. Cut ribbon 1" (2.5 cm) longer than the book cover. Glue the ribbon to the front cover, over the cut edge of the paper near the spine, wrapping the ends to the inside. Repeat on the back cover.

4 Cut two 10" (25.5 cm) lengths of ribbon for ties. Apply glue to 1½" (3.8 cm) of the ribbon end; secure to the center of the inside front cover. Repeat for the inside back cover.

5 Cut two rectangles of paper ¼" (6 mm) smaller than the inside cover. Glue the paper to the inside covers, covering the wrapped extensions and the ribbon ends. Smooth in place with the bone folder.

6 On card stock, make a title card on your computer, or print one in your own handwriting. Cut a rectangle of another color of card stock a scant ⅜" (1 cm) larger than the title card. Punch slots in the corners; mount the title card. Adhere the title to the book front.

Heirloom Christmas Tray

Preserve vintage cards or special Christmas photos under glass in a holiday tray that is sure to become a treasured heirloom. When you pass around the Christmas cookies and hot drinks on this special tray, friends and family receive an extra treat with a blast from the Christmas past that sparks warm memories.

How to Make an Heirloom christmas Tray

You will need:

- Unpainted basswood serving tray (Walnut Hollow #3580)
- Extra-fine sandpaper; tack cloth
- Woodburning pen
- Rubber stamp of holiday motif; ink pad
- Oil color pencils
- Workable fixative; clear wood sealer
- Cotton velveteen fabric
- Liquid fray preventer
- Spray adhesive
- Vintage Christmas cards or Christmas photos
- Window glass cut to the inside bottom measurement of the tray
- Clear acrylic caulk

1 Sand the entire tray, using extra-fine sandpaper. Wipe with a tack cloth. Stamp designs on the tray sides and ends.

2 Read woodburning pen manufacturer's directions carefully. Attach Universal point to wood burning pen; heat pen. Burn lines over stamped design lines. Draw the point steadily toward you at a slow pace, holding the pen lightly. For darker lines, move the pen slower; do not press harder.

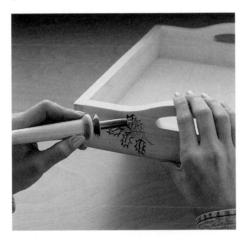

3 Lightly sand away any remaining stamped lines. Color design, using oil color pencils. Shade and highlight the designs as desired. Spray colored areas with workable fixative; allow to dry.

4 Apply two thin coats of water-based varnish over entire tray; allow to dry between coats.

5 Outline a rectangle on the wrong side of the velveteen the same size as the inside tray bottom. Apply a thin line of liquid fray preventer over the line; allow to dry. Cut out the rectangle.

6 Apply spray adhesive to the wrong side of the velveteen; adhere to the inside tray bottom.

7 Make copies of desired cards or photos; arrange them over the velveteen. Clean glass on both sides; place over cards or photos. Apply a thin line of clear acrylic caulk around the outer edge of the glass, sealing the joint between the glass and the wood. Allow to dry.

Decorating with Heirlooms

Toy Horses

Vintage toy horses, perhaps once Christmas presents themselves, are corralled to make an interesting holiday display. Some festive greens and berries, soft candlelight, and a bountiful cluster bow, infuse this gathering with holiday spirit. More than decorative, this nostalgic posse kindles a reverie of a bygone era. One can almost picture the glee in the eyes of the lad who first discovered this rocking horse one Christmas morning years ago.

Cluster bows are easy to make in any size, with any kind of ribbon. Wire-edge ribbons are especially versatile because they can be shaped and arranged into curves and folds that stay where you put them. The key to achieving a luxurious look is to be generous with the ribbon. The size of the bow should be in proportion to the item being embellished. To estimate the ribbon length needed, multiply the desired diameter of the bow by the desired number of loops. Add 6" (15 cm) to this measurement for the center loop plus the desired length for tails and extra streamers. To protect the surface to which you are attaching the bow, use a chenille stem, or pipe cleaner, to hold the loops together at the center.

How to Make a Cluster Bow

You will need:

♦ Ribbon in desired width; calculate length as above
♦ Chenille stem

1 Place the thumb and index finger at the determined length for the tail, with ribbon right side up, if not reversible. Fold the ribbon back on itself at a diagonal, with wrong sides together, forming a right angle.

2 Wrap ribbon over thumb to form center loop; secure with fingers. Twist ribbon one-half turn at underside of loop, so the right side faces up.

3 Form first loop. Twist ribbon one-half turn, and form a loop on the opposite side.

4 Continue forming loops under the previous loops, alternating sides and twisting ribbon after each loop is formed; make each set of loops slightly larger than the set above it. Cut tail to desired length after forming last loop.

5 Insert chenille stem through the center of the bow; twist tightly, gathering ribbon. Cut twisted stem ends short; tuck up inside bow. Separate and shape the loops.

This teapot stands on its own matching base, though a china saucer or dessert plate would work as well. Boxwood and cedar greens inserted into saturated floral foam provide a fragrant, verdant background for showing off the intricate details of the teapot and cups. Roses are inserted into individual water tubes for lasting freshness.

You will need:

- ◆ Floral foam for fresh flowers
- ◆ Low, flat container for holding foam, such as a plastic bowl lid
- ◆ Waterproof floral tape
- ◆ Cedar and boxwood branches
- ◆ Roses
- ◆ Water tubes

- ◆ Small-scale fresh, dried, or artificial white filler material, such as baby's breath or statice
- ◆ Teapot, base or dessert plate, and assorted china teacups
- ◆ Small floating candles

Heirloom China in Centerpiece Displays

Delicate china pieces, collected over the years or passed down from a previous generation, are grouped in an effective holiday centerpiece. Cushioned atop a bed of fresh greens and roses, this elegant teapot evokes memories of a genteel era when afternoon tea was a cherished ritual. A medley of teacups, filled with floating candles, add glimmering light around the base of the arrangement.

How to Arrange an Heirloom China Centerpiece

1 Cut the floral foam 3" (7.5 cm) high to fit the container. Soak the foam in water for at least 20 minutes. Secure the foam to the container, using waterproof floral tape.

2 Cut sprigs of greenery 5" to 8" (12.7 to 20.5 cm) long; trim away any small stems near the ends. Insert two layers of cedar sprigs around the foam sides, near the bottom. Insert boxwood stems into the foam sides, above the cedar stems, filling to the top. Place the teapot base or dessert plate on top of the foam.

3 Cut rose stems diagonally under water, using a sharp knife. Remove any leaves from the stem end. Insert roses into filled water tubes; arrange as desired among the greens.

4 Add small stems of filler flowers sparingly throughout the arrangement. Place floating candles in water-filled teacups; place the cups around the base of the arrangement.

Music Themed Displays

A family heirloom violin is the focal point for a poignant holiday display. Gently cradled on a bed of pine boughs, this beloved instrument wakens joyous memories of its original music maker. The bow, an antique salt cellar, and musical scores are placed on the opposite side of the arrangement to create a sense of balance. Sprigs of holly nestled among other greens add a festive note.

Similar displays can be created with other musical instruments that have special meaning in your family. Use wreaths and fresh-cut boughs as a backdrop, and prop the instrument at an angle in the side foreground of the display. Balance the visual weight of the instrument with smaller items placed on the other side, such as sheet music, smaller instruments, or a metronome.

Vintage Ornaments

Delicate and gently timeworn, vintage ornaments would be lost and unappreciated in a Christmas tree filled with glitzy, glamorous modern-day trinkets. How much more appropriate and favorable it is for them to be displayed on a feather tree! Dangling free in clear view, each fragile ornament flaunts its intricate artistry. One can only marvel at the meticulous care given these beautiful ornaments, to have preserved them unbroken for so many years.

Feather trees originated in Germany in the middle of the 19th century. During a time when the government had banned the cutting of live trees to preserve the German forests, feather trees were improvised as substitute Christmas trees. Dyed goose feathers were twisted around wires and inserted into a wooden trunk that was supported in a painted wooden base. German immigrants brought their feather trees to America, where they became so popular, that by the 1920s they were even being sold in the Sears Roebuck catalogue.

If you are the proud owner of an heirloom feather tree, you no doubt are aware of its value. Because of rekindled interest in feather trees, there are now authentic-looking reproductions available as well as feather tree kits for avid Christmas crafters.

Heritage Dolls

Once the heart of a little girl's universe, vintage dolls are now retired from the toy box and placed on a shelf or in a storage trunk for safekeeping. They are slightly worn from their years of play, perhaps missing a few eyelashes or a button here and there. With pleasant expressions, they seemingly recall hours spent hosting imaginary guests for tea or riding in doll buggies, listening to the chatter of the neighborhood girls.

Christmas, for many heritage dolls, is the anniversary of their entry into the family. As special gifts on long-ago Christmases, they were first introduced to the little girls who would come to treasure them so dearly that they would care for them and keep them forever.

So it is only fitting that these precious keepsakes are arranged in a holiday display. From their perch, they watch the current Christmas morning drama unfold and remember the days when they held center stage.

You will need:

- Oranges
- Pencil
- Whole, stemmed cloves
- Sharp tool, such as an awl or knitting needle

Making the clove-studded pomanders is a time-honored holiday handcraft that can be enjoyed by all ages. If covered entirely with cloves, the fruit may dry out and be used as a fragrant pomander for a year or more. Partially studded in interesting designs, the fruits will likely last a week or two before they become moldy and must be discarded.

How to Make Pomanders

1 Draw the desired design on the orange rind, using a pencil. Use one of our patterns opposite for inspiration or develop one of your own.

2 Poke a hole in the design line, using an awl or knitting needle. Insert a clove into the hole. Repeat until the design is complete, placing cloves as close together as possible.

Copper Collection

A soft patina, earned from hard use and old age, tempers the warm glow of bright copper kettles and colanders. Used in an unexpected holiday display, several pieces are arranged on a table runner with the largest in the forefront, slightly off-center. Nostalgic, clove-studded oranges nestle in a bed of pine sprigs and seeded eucalyptus inside a colander, filling the room with their delicious, spicy fragrance. Snowy paperwhites and hyacinths, forced into winter blooms (page 98), add their fresh two scents to the bouquet. Retired Mason jars complement the warm color scheme with their crystal-clear blue.

Sleigh Bells & Garland

The entry to your home gives your visitors a glimpse into the warmth and hospitality that awaits them inside. Whether it is architecturally astounding or merely ordinary, your entry can welcome holiday guests with generous spirit.

Pillars or posts flanking the front door are perfect for decorating with fresh garland. A strap of rustic sleigh bells peaks through the pine needles on this garland-wrapped post and instantly jingles in the thoughts of passersby. Without hesitation, a familiar Christmas melody pops into their heads. Nearby, the urn that a few short months ago spilled over with summer flowers now boasts a bounty of red berries, dogwood branches, and pine.

To heighten the impact of the garland-wrapped post, a wide red ribbon was first secured to its front. Eye screws, unseen at the top and bottom of the post back, provide a place for anchoring the garland and sleigh bells with wire. A jaunty plaid cluster bow (page 46) is attached at the top, its lanky streamers fluttering in the wind.

Wooden Firkins

Long ago they performed a vital food storage role in daily domestic life. Today, humble, wooden firkins serve a less taxing, ornamental purpose. Stacked in a corner, their varying sizes and colors merely hint at their past usefulness. In honor of their practical nature, these old-time wooden canisters are often taken out of retirement as present-day storage for anything from yarn balls to magazines.

For this holiday display, a firkin that in a past life may have kept the mice away from the family's winter rice ration now holds a fragrant bouquet of pine boughs. In a daydream conceived from this lowly display, one might imagine that old Saint Nicholas once treated his reindeer to a Christmas Eve feast of crunchy carrots and oats served out of a trusty firkin.

A lush, square wreath, brimming with berries and fresh greenery, offers the colorful backdrop for this otherwise spartan display. Realistically, fresh colorful berries on stems are hard to come by in most areas in the winter and would be expensive in the amounts needed to create a wreath like this. However, fresh seeded eucalyptus or fresh juniper, both readily available, can be combined with bright artificial or dried berries to make a wreath that can be stored and reused every year.

You will need:

- Wire wreath frame
- Floral paddle wire
- Pruner
- Fresh seeded eucalyptus or fresh juniper branches with berries
- Dried and artificial berries on stems

How to Make a Berry Wreath

1 Cut eucalyptus stems or juniper branches and assorted berry stems 6" to 8" (15 to 20.5 cm) long. Cluster together several pieces of each element; secure with floral wire. Repeat until you have enough clusters to fill the wreath.

2 Secure the paddle wire to a crossbar on the wire frame. Lay a cluster on the frame and wrap the stems with wire tightly two or three times; do not cut the wire. Place another cluster over the first, with the stems pointing in the same direction and overlapping by half; wrap with wire three times.

3 Repeat step two, overlapping the clusters and staggering them from side to side to fill out the wreath. When you reach the starting point, tuck the stems of the last few clusters under the foliage of the first cluster. Wrap the wire tightly, and cut.

4 Secure a wire loop to the wreath back for hanging, if necessary.

Nostalgic Christmas Postcards

Photographs of your prized antique collections or family heirlooms, arranged in holiday displays, make great Christmas postcards. You can create them on a home computer system that includes basic publishing and image software with a color printer. A scanner is necessary if you are working with actual photographs. You can also use images downloaded into your computer from a digital camera.

A Wish from the Bakers for a Christmas Full of Music and Harmony

May You Have an Old-Fashioned Christmas!
—the Bakers

Wishing you a Christmas rich with love & whimsey!
—the Bakers

How to Create Nostalgic Christmas Postcards

You will need:

- Computer with basic publishing and image software
- Scanner or digital camera
- Color inkjet printer
- White inkjet or all-purpose paper
- Heavy card stock in white or light color

Make a simple hand sketch of your postcard design. Try out different messages and different fonts at about 18 point size. Postcards can range in size from 4" × 6" (10 × 15 cm) to 5½" × 8½" (14 × 21.8 cm). For efficiency, the combined length and width must not exceed 10" (25.5 cm) in order to fit three on a sheet with room for trimming. For best results, photos that are scanned should not be enlarged more than 20% to retain their clarity.

1 Select a developed photo and scan it at 100% at 300 dpi. Or take the picture with a digital camera and download it into your computer. Save the scan or digital image as a TIF in CMYK mode.

2 Create a letter-size document, using publishing software. Using the diagram as a reference, place guides on the page so you have three postcard boxes measuring 3½" × 5" (9 × 12.7 cm).

3 Place an image box inside one guide box. Bring in your scanned image and size it to fit. Place a text box on top of the image and type in your message in the font you have selected; color the font, if desired. If you want a colored box behind the message, place another image box under it. Select a color for the box and add a border color, if desired.

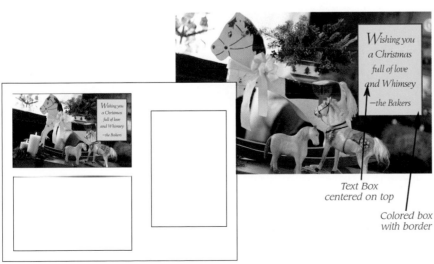

Text Box
centered on top

Colored box
with border

4 If the image doesn't fill the postcard box on all sides, place another image box the full size of the postcard, coloring it "none" with a border or frame of 1 point black. This will give you a trim guide.

May You Have an
Old-Fashioned Christmas!

The Bakers

5 Print out a test of the completed postcard on plain paper; make any necessary changes.

6 Group all the elements of your postcard; copy and paste them into the remaining two guide boxes. Following the diagram, you will have to turn at least one group 90°. Print out another test; make necessary changes.

7 Set up your printer for printing on heavy card stock, following the printer manufacturer's directions. Print the postcards. Cut them to size.

Christmas Memories Shadow Box

If you are lucky enough to have in your possession an heirloom Christmas photograph and a few mementos actually pictured in the photograph, you have the elements for a nostalgic shadow-box display. Shadow boxes have deep sides that allow you to mount dimensional items, such as jewelry, fashion accessories, small toys, and other memorabilia. They are available in many styles, sizes, and finishes and can be ordered in the desired size and depth at framing shops.

Foam-core board, wrapped with fabric, is used for the mounting board at the back of the shadow box and to line the sides of the frame. Items can be stitched or glued to the mounting board or secured with plastic clips designed specifically for that purpose. For conservation-quality framing, use acid-free foam-core board and natural-fiber fabric, such as 100% silk, linen, or cotton.

To determine the shadow box size you need, arrange all the objects to be framed on a sheet of craft paper, making sure to allow the desired amount of space around each item. Mark the frame size and outline the items on the paper to record the placement. To determine the frame depth, measure the deepest item; add 1/2" (1.3 cm) to this measurement to allow for the frame assembly. Order the shadow box and the glass to these measurements or purchase a ready-made one that will work.

You will need:

- Wooden shadow box
- Natural fiber fabric
- 1/4" (6 mm) acid-free foam-core board
- Double-stick framer's tape or adhesive transfer gum (ATG) tape
- Gummed or self-adhesive linen framer's tape
- Clear acrylic finish; paintbrush
- Utility knife; cork-backed metal straightedge
- Needle, thread, fishing line, thimble, clear silicone glue, plastic mounting clips, as needed for mounting various items
- Backing paper
- Framer's fitting tool or slip-joint pliers
- Awl
- 3/4" (2 cm) brads
- Screw eyes
- Hanging wire
- Rubber bumpers

How to Create a Christmas Shadow Box Display

1 Seal any unfinished wood, using clear acrylic finish; allow to dry. Place the glass in the shadow box.

2 Cut two strips of foam-core board 1/8" (3 mm) shorter and narrower than the inside top and bottom dimensions of the shadow box. Cut fabric 2" (5 cm) larger than the strips. Secure double-stick framer's tape to one side of the foam-core strip along the outer edges. Center strip, tape side up, on wrong side of fabric. Wrap fabric firmly around long sides; press in place onto tape.

3 Wrap fabric around ends, folding mitered corners; secure to tape. Secure folded fabric at corners, using strips of linen framer's tape.

4 Place fabric-covered strips into top and bottom of frame; pieces should fit snugly without buckling. Cut strips to fit the sides, and wrap them with fabric in the same way as the top and bottom strips; insert into shadow box.

5 Cut the mounting board 1/4" (6 mm) smaller than the rabbet opening dimensions. Wrap the mounting board with fabric as for the side pieces.

6 Remove the foam-core strips; clean glass on both sides, using glass cleaner and lint-free cloth. Reposition glass in frame. Apply double-stick tape to backs of foam-core strips; reposition top and bottom strips in shadow box, then side strips.

7 Attach items to the mounting board, as shown opposite. Place the mounting board in the frame. Insert 3/4" (2 cm) brads into the middle of each side, using a framer's tool as shown. Or use a slip-joint pliers, protecting the outside edge of the frame with a strip of cardboard. Recheck the display and glass for lint, and remove the brads if necessary to clean the glass.

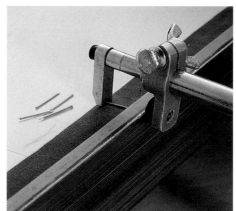

8 Insert brads along each side, 1" (2.5 cm) from the corners and at about 2" (5 cm) intervals. Cut backing paper 2" (5 cm) larger than frame dimensions. Attach double-stick transfer tape to frame back, about 1/8" (3 mm) from outside edges; remove paper covering.

9 Place paper on frame back, stretching it taut. Crease paper over outer edges. Using a straightedge and utility knife, trim paper about 1/8" (3 mm) inside creased line.

10 Mark placement of screw eyes, using an awl, about one-third down from upper edge; secure screw eyes into frame. Thread wire end two or three times through one screw eye; then twist end onto itself. Repeat at opposite side, allowing slack in hanging wire; top of wire is usually 2" to 3" (5 to 7.5 cm) from top of frame when hung.

11 Cover wire ends with masking tape. Secure rubber bumpers to frame back, at lower corners.

Mounting Unframed Photographs and Flat Paper Items

1 Cut stiff mounting board, such as mat board, to the dimensions of the photograph or paper item. Place the item face-down on a smooth, clean surface. Fold a 1¼" (3.2 cm) strip of linen framer's tape, adhesive side out, folding back ¼" to ½" (6 mm to 1.3 cm), depending on the size and weight of the item. Adhere the short side of the tape to the item near one end, with the folded edge of the tape a scant ⅛" (3 mm) below the upper edge of the item. Repeat at the opposite end of same edge. Then repeat at opposite edge.

2 Moisten the free tape ends or remove paper backing; secure the item to the mounting board, aligning the outer edges. Secure the mounted item to the shadow box mounting board in the same way. Or use plastic mounting clips.

Mounting Dimensional Items

Plastic clips: Use plastic clips, available at framing stores. Following the manufacturer's directions, select a clip style that best suits the object.

Hand stitches: Using a thimble and needle threaded with matching thread or monofilament fishing line, secure the item in several places through the mounting board with hand stitches. On the board back, tie the thread tails and secure them to the board with linen framer's tape.

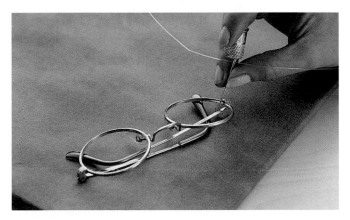

Clear silicone glue: Secure lightweight items to the mounting board with a bead of clear silicone glue. Allow it to dry for 24 hours before placing the mounting board into the frame.

Creating Christmas Traditions

Christmas Memories Album

Looking through old photos of Christmases past is part of the joy of Christmas present. Images of family celebrations, neighborhood get-togethers, holiday choir concerts, or a trip to see Santa Claus rekindle the spirit of the season. An organized photo album, complete with journal entries, is a family treasure that can be enjoyed for many years. An album that showcases your family Christmas photographs can be kept on display throughout the holidays, adding a decorative accent while becoming the focus of every holiday gathering.

Photo album pages can be designed in many ways. Avid scrapbookers add die-cut paper shapes, stickers, and fancy lettering, turning each page into a miniature collage. You may prefer a more classic method, such as simply attaching photos to blank pages and writing a short caption under each. A middle-of-the-road approach could incorporate simple colored paper frames to enhance the photos, with a sprinkling of paper-punched shapes or rubber-stamped images.

There are some basic guidelines to follow that will ensure your album will last for many years and your photos will not be damaged. In creating your album pages, use only papers that are acid-free, lignin-free, and colorfast. Acid causes paper to deteriorate and become brown and brittle over time. Lignin is a substance that causes paper to turn yellow when exposed to light and humidity. Pigments and dyes that are colorfast will not fade over time or exposure to light and will not bleed onto other papers. Ideally, look for albums, pages, and other components that are PAT-approved. This means they have passed the Photographic Activity Test, which assesses the possibility that a photograph could be damaged by coming in contact with the product. Avoid putting adhesives of any kind directly onto original photographs. Instead, secure the photos to the pages, using adhesive photo corners.

Label your photographs to ensure that future generations will be able to identify the subjects. Include names, dates, and information about where the event took place. Whenever possible, use your own handwriting, adding to the value of your photo collection. Use only pens that are labeled to be archivally safe. This means that they are waterproof, fade resistant, permanent, odorless when dry, and quick drying. Never write directly on the image, even if it is a copy. You can label the back of a photograph, taking the precautions of using a soft graphite pencil and placing the photo face-down on a hard surface, to prevent indentations.

Sheet protectors are another good investment. These clear plastic covers slip onto the pages, either from the side or the top, protecting the images from abrasion as the pages rub together. Some styles have pockets for photographs and captions, so no paper backing pages are really necessary. Be sure to use only page protectors that are made of polyester or polypropylene to ensure that they will not deteriorate over time or damage your photos.

It is wise to create the entire Christmas album from copies of your photographs, keeping the originals in safe storage. Duplicate copies for each child in the family will be very much appreciated when your children become adults and move away from home.

For our Christmas album, we chose a sturdy, hinged wooden cover by Walnut Hollow. The wood is smooth and ready to decorate. Wood itself contains acid and lignin, so be sure to seal it with a clear acrylic sealer and insert protective pages between the covers and photo pages.

How to Mount Photos

Photo corners: Use acid-free, lignin-free adhesive photo corners to attach photos to the pages.

Paper frames: Cut a paper rectangle in a color that will accent the photo, a scant 3⁄8" (1 cm) larger than the photo. Use a corner slot punch to cut corner slits to hold the photo. Insert the photo. Adhere the colored rectangle to the album page.

Clear pages: Insert photos and handwritten captions into the divided polypropylene pages.

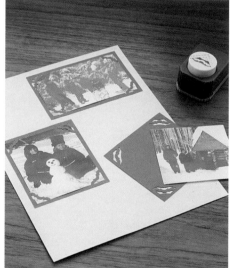

How to Make a Christmas Photo Album Cover

You will need:

♦ Hinged wooden album cover by Walnut Hollow
♦ Fine sandpaper; tack cloth
♦ Woodburning pen with calligraphy and mini-flow points
♦ Graphite transfer paper
♦ Decorative pressed wood corners
♦ Water-based gel stains in red and green
♦ Wood glue
♦ Clear acrylic finish

1 Remove the hinges and binding posts from the cover. Sand all surfaces smooth, using fine sandpaper; wipe with a tack cloth. Transfer the title design from page 107 to the center of the front cover, using graphite paper.

2 Using a calligraphy point, woodburn the title into the cover. Hold the pen consistently at the same angle to create the narrow and wide areas of the letters. Move the pen very slowly, applying only light pressure to the wood.

3 Lightly write, "Created by (your name)" along with the date on the back of the front cover, using a graphite pencil. Woodburn over the letters, using the mini-flow point.

4 Stain the pressed wood corners in red and green, following the manufacturer's directions. Allow to dry.

5 Adhere the pressed wood corners to the cover, using wood glue. Allow to dry.

6 Apply two coats of clear acrylic sealer to all wood surfaces, allowing to dry between coats.

7 Reassemble the covers, inserting a stack of album pages with protective sleeves.

Add-a-Charm Christmas Stocking

The hanging of the Christmas stockings is a traditional activity that truly marks the season for children and adults alike. As symbols of anticipation and promise, personalized Christmas stockings become treasured keepsakes. Some may accompany their keepers when they leave the family nest; others continue to occupy their space on the homestead mantel. This unique version comes with its own tradition and promise. Every year a new charm will be given, perhaps as a stocking stuffer gift, to be tacked onto the Christmas tree appliqué. As the child grows, his stocking tree fills with ornament tokens.

How to Make an Add-a-Charm Stocking

You will need:

- ¾ yd. (0.7 m) fabric for stocking
- 1 yd. (0.92 m) fabric for lining, cuff, and hanger
- ¾ yd. (0.7 m) low-loft batting
- Temporary spray adhesive
- ¼ yd. (0.25 m) fusible interfacing
- Scrap fabrics for appliqués
- Paper-backed fusible web
- Narrow ribbons for tree garland and gifts
- Tear-away stabilizer
- Thread to match stocking fabric and appliqués
- Charms

1 Enlarge the stocking pattern on page 108. With fabric folded right sides together, cut two stocking pieces from outer fabric and two from lining. Cut two stocking pieces from batting. For the cuff, cut a 7" × 17" (18 × 43 cm) rectangle from cuff fabric and interfacing. Cut a 2" × 8" (5 × 20.5 cm) piece for the hanger.

2 Trace the tree, trunk, and gift appliqué shapes from the patterns on pages 108–109 onto the paper backing of fusible web; cut apart, leaving small margins. Fuse onto appliqué fabrics, following the manufacturer's directions. Cut out appliqués.

3 Lightly mark placement lines for gift ribbons and tree garland. Remove paper backing from appliqués. Following the placement guide, fuse the pieces onto the stocking front.

4 Apply the batting to the wrong side of the stocking pieces, using temporary spray adhesive. Place tear-away stabilizer under the stocking front. Stitch around each appliqué, using satin stitch (short, narrow zigzag). Straight stitch narrow ribbon over the marked lines. Remove stabilizer.

5 Pin stocking pieces right sides together. Stitch ½" (1.3 cm) seam around stocking, leaving top open. Trim seam allowances; clip curves. Repeat for lining.

6 Turn stocking right side out; press lightly. Insert lining into stocking, aligning seams. Baste lining to stocking around the top within seam allowance.

7 Fold the hanger in half, lengthwise, right sides together. Stitch ¼" (6 mm) seam, leaving open at ends. Turn right side out and press. Fold hanger in half and baste to upper edge of stocking at back seam.

8 Fuse the interfacing to the wrong side of the cuff, following the manufacturer's directions. Fold the cuff in half crosswise, right sides together. Stitch ½" (1.3 cm) seam, forming a circle; press seam open. Fold the cuff in half, wrong sides together; press.

9 Pin the cuff to the lining side of the stocking top. Stitch ½" (1.3 cm) seam; trim. Turn cuff to outside of stocking.

Christmas Eve Pillowcase

With all the excitement and anticipation on Christmas Eve, how is a little one supposed to sleep? Sweet slumber comes easily when your cherub is tucked under the covers between cozy flannel sheets with her head resting on a magic Christmas pillowcase. You create the magic with a sprinkling of Christmas appliqués and a healthy dose of love in every stitch.

How to Make a Christmas Eve Pillowcase

You will need:

♦ 1 yd. (0.92 m) red flannel fabric

♦ ¼ yd. (0.25 m) white flannel fabric

♦ ½ yd. (0.5 m) red-and-white striped cotton fabric

♦ ¼ yd. (0.25 m) light brown cotton fabric

♦ Sewing machine

♦ Cotton machine embroidery thread

♦ Paper-backed fusible web

♦ Iron

♦ Fabric markers in black and red

♦ White baby rickrack

1 Prewash all fabrics. Cut a rectangle of red flannel 40½" × 27" (103 × 68.5 cm) for pillowcase body. Cut a rectangle of white flannel 40½" × 10" (103 × 25.5 cm) for the pillowcase hem. For the flat piping trim, cut two strips of red-and-white striped fabric on the true bias, 2" (5 cm) wide; piece strips for a continuous length of 40½" (103 cm).

2 Trace and cut out the patterns on page 110. Apply paper-backed fusible web to the wrong side of appliqué fabrics, following the manufacturer's directions. Trace patterns on paper backing; take care that candy canes are aligned with the fabric bias.

3 Cut out designs; remove paper backing. Fold red fabric in half, wrong sides together. Position appliqués on pillowcase front, following placement guide; fuse.

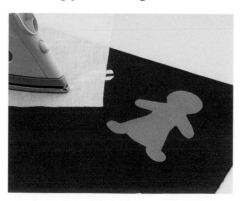

4 Open the fabric. Stitch rickrack onto cookie shapes. Draw faces and buttons with fabric markers. Satin-stitch around appliqués, using cotton embroidery thread in the sewing machine. Place tear-away stabilizer under the fabric to prevent puckering. Remove the stabilizer after stitching.

5 Press the hem in half, lengthwise, wrong sides together. Then fold in half crosswise. Repeat steps 2 to 4 for the letters of the child's name, centering them on the hem front. If your sewing machine has embroidery capability, program it to stitch the words "Sweet Dreams" or "Hurry Santa" repeatedly just above the hem fold; follow your sewing machine guide.

6 Press the piping strip in half, wrong sides together, taking care not to distort the width. Pin the piping strip to one long edge of the pillowcase body, aligning raw edges. Baste within the ½" (1.3 cm) seam allowance.

7 Press under ½" (1.3 cm) on front long edge of hem. Pin other edge, right side down, to the wrong side of the pillowcase. Stitch ½" (1.3 cm) seam.

8 Press seam allowances toward hem. Wrap hem to right side, just covering stitching line with folded edge. Topstitch close to fold.

9 Stitch pillowcase end and side seams, using ½" (1.3 cm) seam allowance. Serge seam allowances together, trimming to ¼" (6 mm). Or trim seam allowances to ¼" (6 mm) and zigzag.

Countdown Christmas Tree

Waiting for Christmas is a tough assignment for little ones, especially when they haven't quite grasped the concept of time. A countdown tree helps kids look forward to Christmas, with a tiny surprise every day in December. Twenty-four ornaments, each tucked away in its own numbered package, are stacked beneath a miniature tree. Day by day the packages are opened and the wee ornaments inside are hung on the tree. By the time Christmas arrives, the tree is decked out in a brilliant display of color. On Christmas day, package number 25 is opened to reveal the star that tops off the tree with perfection.

Children enjoy decorating their own pint-sized fresh-cut, or potted countdown tree. If you prefer, a small imitation fir tree can be stored along with the boxed ornaments year to year. Small papier-mâché boxes with lids, available at craft stores, are the perfect sizes for various small ornaments, which can be handmade or purchased.

How to Prepare the Boxes for the Countdown Tree

1 Paint all surfaces of the box and lid, using desired color of acrylic craft paint. Allow to dry. Poke a small hole in the center of the lid, using an awl. Paint bow loops around the hole, using gold or silver paint pen; paint ribbons on the rest of the lid and box.

2 Thread decorative cording onto a darning needle. Run the needle through the button, through the lid from the underside, through the gift tag, back through the lid, and back through the button. Knot the cording ends together under the button so the cording forms a small loop in the center of the painted bow. Secure button to underside of lid, using hot glue.

3 Repeat steps 1 and 2 for all the boxes. Apply adhesive numbers 1 through 25 to the gift tags. Place a little shredded paper in the bottom of each box. Place one miniature ornament in each box, 1 through 24.

4 Paint the star as desired; allow to dry. Drill two small holes, 1/4" (6 mm) apart, near the star center. Cut a 10" (25.5 cm) length of gold craft wire. Insert one end of the wire through the holes; twist to secure on the back. Beginning from the opposite end, wrap the remaining wire around a pencil. Remove the wire from the pencil and gently unwind from the open end, creating a cone-shaped spiral for mounting the star. Place the star in box number 25.

You will need:

- Assortment of 24 purchased or handmade miniature ornaments
- 24 small papier-mâché boxes
- 24 small buttons
- Awl
- Small wooden star
- Drill and small bit
- Gold craft wire
- Acrylic craft paints
- Gold and silver paint pens
- Artist's brushes
- Craft glue; hot glue gun
- ½" (1.3 cm) adhesive numbers
- Sturdy gift tags
- Narrow decorative cording
- Darning needle
- Shredded colored paper

Making Family Christmas Cards

The holidays are a popular time for corresponding with family and friends, for catching up on life events, and for extending wishes for happiness and good will. In this world of mass production, handmade Christmas cards are an expression of extra thoughtfulness. They need not be particularly artistic or elaborate to convey their personal message. Crafting the annual Christmas card can become a valued family tradition, even in families where other handcrafts and hobbies are not pursued.

There are many paper options and creative techniques for making Christmas cards. Start with blank cards or create your own from card or paper stock, available from stationery, art, or craft stores. Print your cover greeting first, either by hand or with a rubber stamp or on your home computer. Print the inner message on the card or on a separate piece of paper to be inserted later in one of several clever ways. Then embellish the cards as lavishly or as simply as you wish. Consider a variety of effects, including pressure embossing, stamping, thermal embossing, and stenciling. Create interest with layered shapes, decorative edges, cutout designs, interesting folds, and punched shapes. Incorporate

other elements, such as ribbons, preserved greenery, or holiday trims. To display a snapshot, plan a cutout or use paper photo frames or corners suitable for scrapbooking.

Craft stores and paper specialty stores are full of products and tools that can be used to make Christmas cards: stickers, die-cut paper shapes, paper photo frames, hole punches, adhesives and tapes, watercolor markers, gel roller pens, pastels, colored pencils, decorative-blade scissors, rubber stamping materials, brass embossing plates, stencils, ribbons, and other trims.

Folding Basics

Text-weight paper can usually be creased successfully in both directions. Heavier papers, however, should be indented or scored before creasing, to ensure a smooth folded edge.

Indenting: Lightly mark the intended fold line on the inside of the fold. Align a metal ruler to the line. Indent the line, sliding a fine-point stylus or a dull table knife along the ruler edge. Fold the paper with the indented line on the inside.

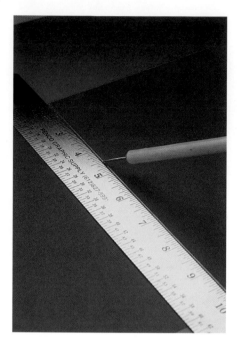

Scoring: Lightly mark the intended fold line on the outside of the fold. Align a metal ruler to the line. Holding a craft knife with the blade facing upward, score the line, sliding the knife tip along the ruler edge and cutting gently through only the upper layer of fibers. Fold the paper with the scored line on the outside.

Pressure Embossing

You will need:

- ◆ Card stock or medium-weight paper
- ◆ Embossing plate
- ◆ Ball-tip stylus
- ◆ Removable tape
- ◆ Light box or other illuminated glass surface

1 Tape the embossing plate to the light box or an illuminated glass surface. Place the card, wrong side up, over the embossing plate in the desired position. Tape the card edges down, using removable tape. Test the tape on a scrap of paper first, to be sure it won't damage the card.

2 Trace around the outside of all the design areas with the stylus, applying firm pressure. If the stylus squeaks during use, lubricate the end by rubbing it in the palm or your hand. Remove the tape.

Stamped Designs

You will need:

- Ink pad
- Rubber stamp
- Watercolor markers, colored pencils, or pastels

1 Press the stamp firmly onto the stamp pad; lift and repeat as necessary until the rubber design is coated with ink. Avoid getting any ink on the flat surface surrounding the design.

2 Press the stamp straight down onto the card front, using firm, even pressure. Lift the stamp straight up to remove it. Allow ink to dry.

3 Color in the stamped design, using watercolor markers, colored pencils, or pastels.

Stenciling

You will need:

- Purchased stencil or paper punches and blank stencil plastic
- Ink pads in desired colors
- Makeup sponges
- Removable tape

1 To make a framed stencil, mark the desired shape on stencil plastic, allowing at least 1" (2.5 cm) around the perimeter. Cut on the marked line, using a mat knife and cutting board; take care not to overcut the corners. To complete the frame, cut again 1" (2.5 cm) beyond the outer edge.

2 Punch designs in the inner stencil, using paper punches. For interest, punch one or two whole shapes toward the center and some smaller, partial shapes along the edges.

3 Secure the stencil frame to the card, using removable tape. Press the sponge onto the ink pad several times. Apply ink lightly to the stencil opening, using a pouncing motion; replenish ink as needed. Allow to dry. Do not remove frame.

4 Secure punched stencil over background, inside frame. Stencil designs. Use a new sponge for every additional color. Remove stencils, allow to dry thoroughly.

Thermal Embossing

You will need:

- Rubber stamp
- Embossing ink pad
- Embossing powder
- Artist's paintbrush
- Heat source, such as a heat tool or light bulb. (Do not use a hair dryer.)

1 Follow steps 1 and 2 for stamping, but do not wait for the ink to dry. Sprinkle the design with embossing powder while the ink is still wet, covering it completely; pour off the excess powder for reuse. Brush away tiny amounts of unwanted powder, using a small artist's paintbrush.

2 Heat the powder with a heat tool or hold the card near a heat source, such as a light bulb, until all the powder melts, forming a raised design.

Photo Fold-out Card

You will need:

- Card stock
- Coordinating paper for photo frame
- Craft knife or scissors
- Ballpoint stylus
- Metal ruler
- 4" × 6" (10 × 15 cm) photo
- Corner slot punch

1 Cut an 8½" (21.8 cm) card stock square. Measure 3½" (9 cm) from the corner on two adjacent sides; mark a point ¼" (6 mm) from the edge. Repeat for the opposite corner. Depending on the thickness of the card, score or indent (page 78) a rectangle connecting the marked points; run the stylus or knife tip through the marks to the card edges. Cut away the small triangles formed at each corner.

2 Decorate the inside of the card as desired; write your greeting on one of the larger flaps, which will be at the top and bottom of the card. Remember scored lines are on the outside; indented lines are on the inside.

3 Trim the photo to an exact 4" × 6" (10 × 15 cm). Cut a coordinating paper frame a scant ⅜" (1 cm) larger than the photo. Punch frame corners with a corner slot punch. Mount the photo in the frame; secure to the center of the card.

4 Fold in the side flaps first, the bottom flap second, and the top flap last; crease each fold sharply. Secure the flaps with a purchased sticker, or make one in a motif to match the card and affix it with double-stick tape.

Cutouts

You will need:

- Craft knife; cutting mat
- Embossing plate, rubber stamp, or stencil, if desired
- Straightedge

1 If part of the cutout will follow the outer edges of an embossed, stamped, or stenciled design, or a row of stickers, apply that design first. Lightly trace the shape of the cutout.

2 Place the card over a cutting mat. Cut out the desired area, using a craft knife, pulling the knife toward you as you cut. Use a straightedge to cut straight lines.

Woven Ribbon

You will need:

- ♦ Ribbon
- ♦ Straightedge
- ♦ Hole punch (rectangular or round)
- ♦ Pencil, white eraser
- ♦ Tape; double-stick foam tape

1 Mark a light pencil line on the back of the overlay where woven ribbon is desired; mark an even number of evenly spaced holes along the line, about 1/2" (1.3 cm) apart. For a bow, center two marks on one side of the overlay, 1/2" (1.3 cm) apart.

2 Punch holes at marks, using a paper punch large enough to accommodate the ribbon. Align all holes to the marked line. Erase pencil lines.

3 Weave ribbon through holes. Secure ends to underside of card, using tape. Tie a bow. To accommodate thickness of ribbon, secure overlay to card, using double-stick foam tape.

Exploding Fold-out Letter

You will need:

- ♦ Standard 4¼" × 5½" (10.8 × 14 cm) single-fold card
- ♦ Text-weight paper, 8½" (21.8 cm) square, printed with desired message

1 Place the paper, face down, with text running in the same direction that the card will open. Fold top down; crease in center. Turn the paper face up. Fold diagonally, aligning corners. Unfold and repeat in opposite direction; unfold, forming an X of valley folds. Horizontal fold is now a mountain fold.

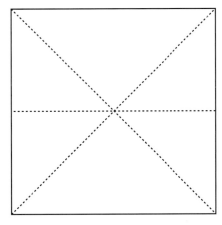

2 Refold the valley folds and bring the ridges of the mountain fold together in the center between the top and bottom layers, forming a triangle.

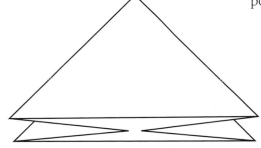

3 Fold the lower points of the top layer toward each other, so points touch at the center of the open edges; crease. Flip the paper over and repeat with the remaining two open points.

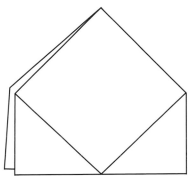

4 Open the paper. Push the folded corners to the inside, reversing the original directions of the folds; crease. Refold the paper.

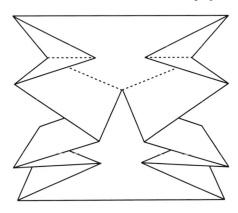

5 Glue the "house-shaped" sections to the inside center of the card, aligning the center point with the card's center fold.

Christmas Card Album

Your family's hand-crafted Christmas cards are a keepsake for you as well as for those on your mailing list. Because they often include a short letter or a family snapshot, your cards are like chapters in your family storybook, and a copy of each should be kept in an archival quality album to be enjoyed through the years.

You will need:

- Binder-style album
- Heavyweight decorative paper or fabric
- 2 yd. (1.85 m) ivory wire-edge ribbon, 1½" (39 mm) wide
- Thin cardboard
- Craft glue
- Rubber stamps of seasonal greetings
- Pigment ink
- Gold embossing powder
- Heat tool
- Heavy gold paper; ivory card stock

How to Make a Card Album

1 Cover the album with heavy decorative paper, following steps 1 to 8 on pages 92 and 93. Wrap front cover vertically with a length of ribbon; knot ends above center and trim short. Make a cluster bow (page 46) with remaining ribbon; tie over knot, leaving 3" to 4" (7.5 to 10 cm) tails.

2 Cut heavy gold paper 3" × 4½" (7.5 × 11.5 cm). Cut ivory card 2½" × 4" (6.5 × 10 cm). Stamp and emboss (page 79) a greeting on the ivory card; sign your family name in permanent marker. Glue the ivory card to the center of the gold paper. Glue the title card to the album cover, as if it were attached to the bow.

3 Stamp and emboss other seasonal greetings on the album cover, as desired.

Autographed Christmas Tablecloth

*W*hen your family and special guests sit down for Christmas dinner, they will find each place setting meticulously appointed as usual. Christmas china, flanked by sparkling flatware, is carefully arranged over a festive bordered tablecloth. To everyone's surprise, your table greeting includes, "Please autograph the tablecloth!" Fine-tip permanent fabric markers are passed around so each guest can sign and date the tablecloth. In the years that follow, this special tablecloth becomes a visual record of past holiday feasts; who attended, where they sat. Special remembrances are sure to follow, providing unending topics for pleasant Christmas table talk.

This tablecloth, which features a 4" (10 cm) mitered border, has a drop length of 10" (25.5 cm). Fine cotton or cotton blend fabric that is tightly woven to produce a smooth finish provides the best surface for writing. Permanent pens that are intended for writing on fabric ensure that the names will remain legible year after year.

You will need:

- Smooth, washable, tightly woven cotton or cotton blend fabric for the center panel; 54" to 60" (137 to 152.5 cm) wide
- Washable Christmas print or plaid fabric for the mitered border
- Straightedge with 45° angle marking
- Thread
- Sewing machine

How to Make an Autograph Tablecloth

1 Preshrink the fabrics by machine washing and drying. Cut the center panel 13" (33 cm) longer and wider than the tabletop. Mark a dot 1/2" (1.3 cm) from each corner. Cut 9" (23 cm) strips of border fabric on the lengthwise grain, cutting them 12" (30.5 cm) longer than the center panel sides and ends.

2 Fold one end of one border strip in half. Cut the end at a 45° angle; unfold. Mark dots on 1/2" (1.3 cm) seamline at outer corners and at pivot point.

3 Mark dots on opposite end of strip a distance from the first dots equal to the distance between corresponding dots on the center panel. Using angled end as a guide and aligning dots, angle-cut the other end.

4 Repeat steps 2 and 3 for each border strip. Pin two adjacent border strips right sides together, matching dots. Stitch 1/2" (1.3 cm) seam between dots, pivoting at point and backstitching at corner dots. Trim seam allowances to 1/4" (6 mm); trim across point diagonally. Press seam allowances open. Repeat for each corner, joining strips into a large circle.

5 Press under 1/2" (1.3 cm) on one continuous edge of the border. Pin the right side of the other raw edge to the wrong side of the center panel; match dots and align edges. Stitch 1/2" (1.3 cm) seam on each side, pivoting at each corner dot.

6 Press the seam toward the border. Turn the border to the right side of the tablecloth so the inner fold covers the seam; pin. Edgestitch close to the inner fold.

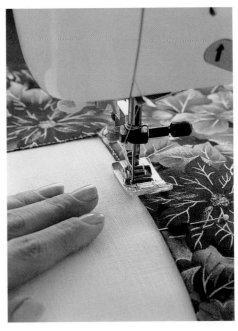

Christmas Grow Chart

A personal record of a child's growth, accompanied by snap shots and brief journal notes about the year's major accomplishments or favorite activities, are all tied up in a neat little package. Every Christmas, when it's time to decorate the tree or bake Christmas cookies, it's also time to mark the child's height and add to the mini-memoirs in this accordion-folded booklet.

How to Make a christmas Grow Chart

To hang the grow chart for measuring, form a loop with the ribbon tails. Fold and tie the chart into a small booklet, and hang it as an ornament on the tree, making it a lasting Christmas keepsake.

You will need:

♦ Cardboard
♦ Decorative paper or sturdy wrapping paper with a Christmas theme
♦ 30" (76 cm) ribbon, 5/8" (15 mm) wide
♦ High quality art paper, 19" × 25" (48.5 × 63.5 cm)
♦ Paper cutter, scissors, or rotary cutter and mat
♦ Craft glue
♦ Rubber stamps and stamp pads or stickers with a Christmas theme
♦ Heavy paper, for title card
♦ Scissors with decorative blades

1 Cut two 4" (10 cm) squares of cardboard for the chart covers. Cut two 5" (12.7 cm) squares of decorative paper. Lightly draw 1/2" (1.3 cm) squares on the wrong side of the paper in each corner. Cut away each corner, cutting from just outside the lines to the point. Apply glue to the wrong side of the paper. Glue paper onto covers.

2 Place the the ribbon over the wrong side of one cover, with the ribbon center at the lower edge; glue in place.

3 Cut two 3¾" (9.5 cm) strips of high quality art paper, cutting in the lengthwise direction. Mark faint pencil lines across the strips every 3¾" (9.5 cm). Trim off the last short section of the first strip ¼" (6 mm) beyond the line. Glue the second strip to the first, lapping it up to the line. Trim off the last short section of the second strip.

4 Accordion-fold the pieced strip, folding on the lines. Glue the end squares to the unfinished sides of the covers, so the lengthwise direction of the paper is parallel to the ribbon. Align the upper edge of the strip to the edge of the cover with the shorter ribbon tail.

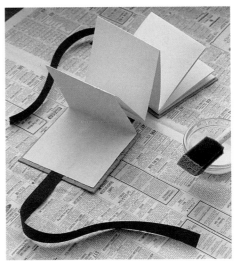

5 Decorate the grow chart with rubber stamped images or stickers, if desired. Make a title plate, using a rectangle of heavy paper. Trim the edges, using scissors with decorative blades; glue the title plate to the outside of the cover that holds the ribbon. Fold it up, wrap the ribbon around the booklet, and tie a bow along the upper edge.

Santa Cookie Plate

Your children's artwork, though naive and unskilled, becomes more precious as time goes on. With the capabilities of color printers or home computers, you and your kids can create a Santa cookie plate that features their own paintings or drawings, while preserving the original artwork. No matter what size the original art is, it can be scaled to fit the size of the plate. Individual elements of a design can be resized and copied in multiples, if necessary. Santa will get a real kick out of eating his cookies from this plate every Christmas, and long after the tradition has been left behind, the plate will still prompt smiles of remembrance.

You will need:

- Clear glass plate
- Children's Christmas artwork
- Access to color printer or home computer with scanner and printer
- Scissors with fine, sharp blades and point
- Fine point marking pens, optional
- Decoupage medium
- Brush or sponge applicator
- Acrylic paints
- Sea sponge
- Aerosol acrylic sealer

1 Copy your child's Christmas art on a color copier or scan and print it, using your home computer; resize the picture as necessary to fit the plate. Reproduce certain elements of the design to use in multiples, if desired.

2 Cut out individual design motifs, using scissors with fine, sharp blades and points. Outline designs with a marking pen, if necessary.

3 Trace the plate on a piece of paper; plan the placement of the design motifs. Clean the back of the plate thoroughly, using glass cleaner and a lint-free cloth; place the plate face-down on the table.

4 Apply a thin layer of decoupage medium to the front of the central motif, using a sponge applicator. Position the motif on the plate back; smooth out any bubbles or wrinkles, using a dampened sponge. Repeat until all motifs are in place; allow to dry completely.

5 Apply a thin coat of decoupage medium to the back of the motifs as a sealer; allow to dry. (Any excess decoupage medium around the edges will not show when the plate is painted.)

6 Apply acrylic paint sparingly, using a sea sponge. Allow to dry. Apply one or two more different colors of sponged paint. If desired, paint the entire plate back a solid color, using an aerosol acrylic paint. Allow to dry.

7 Personalize the plate back with the child's signature and date, using a permanent marking pen. Apply two light coats of aerosol acrylic sealer, drying between coats.

Dear Santa Album

Jolly Old Saint Nick is a big part of Christmas for little kids. The annual visit to the mall to sit on Santa's lap is memorialized in classic Christmas movies, and posing for a picture with Santa is a yearly tradition that dates back at least to the early '50s. Chubby little hands are busy from Thanksgiving to December 24 creating primitive pictures that tell sleigh ride stories. Precious letters to Santa from his short, awe-struck believers are so candid and full of innocence. Even little squirts, before they know how to spell, whittle away at a catalog with their safety scissors and paste together a picture collage of their Christmas wishes. This Dear Santa album captures those priceless photos, letters, and artwork for safekeeping so that, long after the Santa secret is revealed, the magic can be relived in a walk through the pages.

How to Make a Dear Santa Album

You will need:

- Binder-style album
- Red and green plaid fabric
- Thin cardboard
- Craft glue
- Red and green card stock
- Lucite magnetic photo frame
- Self-adhesive acrylic discs
- Hot glue gun or other strong adhesive for plastic
- Wooden letters spelling "DEAR SANTA"
- Red acrylic craft paint

1 Cut a fabric strip with the length equal to the height of the album plus 3" (7.5 cm). For an album with centered rings, the cut width is equal to the width of the spine plus 3" (7.5 cm). For an album with rings attached to the back cover, cut width is equal to the width of the spine plus width of ring base plus 3" (7.5 cm). On back of strip, mark size and location of ring base, keeping 1½" (3.8 cm) margin. Cut through center of marked rectangle, stopping ½" (1.3 cm) from ends; clip diagonally to corners or curves.

2 Fold fabric under, along marked lines. Apply diluted glue sparingly to album, over area to be covered. Secure fabric over ring base; smooth out over spine and onto inside covers. Wrap and secure fabric to outside at top and bottom.

3 Cut fabric 4" (10 cm) larger than open album. Center open album on wrong side of fabric. For album with centered rings, clip fabric to album edge at top and bottom folds of spine. For album with rings attached to back cover, clip to front fold of spine and to right side of ring base.

4 Fold fabric in between clips so raw edges meet album edges. Fold over again, tucking folded edge to outside. Glue fabric to outer album surface.

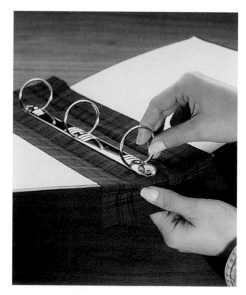

5 Fold fabric to inside at corners; glue in place. Close album to make sure fabric is not too tight. Fold fabric on three edges of each cover to inside, mitering corners and folding fabric diagonally away from clips; glue in place.

7 Apply diluted glue to front cardboard; center fabric over cardboard, and smooth to edges. Fold fabric to back at corners; glue in place. Fold fabric on edges to back, mitering corners; glue in place. Repeat for back cardboard.

10 Remove the magnetic strips from the back of the frame. Spread frame apart slightly; attach clear acrylic discs to the top front surface of the frame back. Secure the frame to the center of the papers, using hot glue or a strong adhesive. Make a copy of a favorite Santa photo; trim to frame size and insert.

11 Paint the letters red; allow to dry. Apply aerosol clear acrylic finish; allow to dry. Arrange the letters in an arc above the frame; adhere, using craft glue.

6 Cut two pieces of lightweight cardboard ⅜" (1 cm) smaller than inside covers. For album with rings attached to back cover, measure for back piece from right side of ring base. Cut two fabric pieces 4" (10 cm) larger than cardboard.

8 Center cardboard pieces over inside covers; glue in place. Close album, and allow to dry thoroughly.

9 Cut red card rectangle 1" (2.5 cm) larger than the lucite frame, using a deckle-blade scissors; cut green card rectangle ½" (1.3 cm) larger than frame. Glue the red rectangle to the center of the album cover. Glue the green rectangle to the center of the red rectangle.

Pass-it-on Gift Box

This handsome, sturdy Christmas gift box carries with it a history and a trust. Whoever receives a gift in it must place a gift inside the following year to give to someone else. As the box is passed from person to person, the giver's greeting, the receiver's name, and what they received are recorded in a special notebook kept inside the cover.

Get the kids to help you decorate the box, or make it yourself and surprise someone the first Christmas. Keep it circulating within your immediate family or include other close relatives and friends with whom you usually celebrate. To make the experience even more special, you may want to stipulate that the gift must be handmade by the giver.

How to Make a Pass-it-on Gift Box

You will need:

- Wooden box with hinged cover
- Small, flat wooden cutouts, such as snowmen and snowflakes
- Fine-grain sandpaper; tack cloth
- Primer for wood
- Painter's masking tape
- Acrylic craft paints; paintbrushes
- Wood glue
- Suede paper
- Clear acrylic sealer
- Heavy card stock
- Small notebook
- Basswood, 1/16" (1.5 mm) thick

Unpainted wooden boxes and small wooden cutouts are available at hobby and craft stores. You can decorate your gift box in a snowman theme like ours, or select other cutouts and a different color scheme to create your own design.

1 Sand all wooden surfaces smooth, using fine-grain sandpaper; wipe with a tack cloth. Prime all surfaces.

2 Mask off the lid knob, if it will be a different color than the lid, and the hinges. Paint the outside of the box, including the upper edge, and all surfaces of the lid as desired; allow to dry. Add coats as necessary, allowing the paint to dry between coats.

3 Remove masking tape from the knob and hinges. Mask off the area around the knob, and paint the knob. Allow to dry; remove masking tape.

4 Paint one side and the narrow edge of the wooden cutouts as desired; allow to dry. Adhere cutouts to the outside of the box, using wood glue.

5 Cut two pieces of suede paper ¼" (6 mm) wider than the inside box depth; cut one to fit the length of two sides, cut the other ½" (1.3 cm) longer than the length of the remaining two sides. On the lower edge of each piece, mark the locations of the box corners with ¼" (6 mm) clips; the outer clips on the longer piece should be ¼" (6 mm) from the ends. Crease the width of the paper at each clip; fold the lower edges in ¼" (6 mm). Apply diluted craft glue to the wrong side of the paper, and secure to the inside of the box, aligning the unclipped edge to the box top and lapping the clipped edge onto the box bottom.

6 Cut a rectangle of suede paper ⅛" (3 mm) smaller than the inside box bottom. Apply diluted craft glue to the wrong side of the paper; adhere to the inside box bottom.

7 Cut a rectangle of 1/16" (1.5 mm) basswood for the notebook retainer, with the length equal to the inside width of the box lid and the width equal to two-thirds the width of the notebook. Cut decorative paper the same length as the retainer, with the width equal to twice the retainer width plus ¼" (6 mm).

8 Apply diluted craft glue to the wrong side of the paper. Center the retainer on the paper and wrap, overlapping the edges on the center of the retainer back.

9 Cut two strips of basswood ⅛" (3 mm) narrower than the inside lip of the box lid, ¼" (6 mm) shorter than the width of the retainer. Using wood glue, adhere the strips to the inside lip of the box lid, abutting the ends to the hinged edge and the back edges to the lid underside.

10 Adhere the retainer to the front edges of the basswood strips, using wood glue; place the seam toward the back. Allow to dry.

11 Decorate the notebook cover as desired, referring to the methods on pages 34, 41, 82, or 92. Slip the notebook inside the lid, behind the retainer.

Forcing Bulbs for Holiday Blooms

Colorful flowers are a refreshing surprise at Christmastime, reminding us of spring's promise in the dead of winter. In a season already charged with anticipation, the tradition of forcing bulbs into holiday blooms is indeed a lesson in patience that pays off with a beautiful, fragrant display.

Traditional holiday favorites are the large, showy amaryllis, shown here, and paperwhite narcissus, shown opposite. They are also the easiest to bring into bloom. Neither of them requires a period of cold storage, and they will bloom within weeks of planting. Amaryllis bulbs usually bloom in six to eight weeks; paperwhites bloom within three to four weeks. With proper care, amaryllis bulbs can be kept and brought into bloom again the following Christmas.

Hyacinth and crocus bulbs, as well as tulips and daffodils, must have a period of artificial winter to enable their root systems to develop. After potting, these bulbs must be kept at 40°F (4°C) for six to fifteen weeks, depending on the variety. A refrigerator is usually the best place to store them, if you have the room. Preconditioned bulbs purchased from a garden center must still be chilled, but for a shorter period of time. Without this cold storage period, their growth and blooms will be stunted.

Purchase bulbs from a nursery or garden center, and follow their recommendations for planting and care. Here are some general guidelines for growing amaryllis and paper white bulbs.

How to Grow Amaryllis

You will need:

- Amaryllis bulb
- Pot, about 2" (5 cm) larger in diameter and several inches deeper than the bulb
- Potting soil
- Water

1 Fill the pot with soil and place the bulb in the pot so that the neck of the bulb will remain exposed. Firm the soil around the bulb.

2 Moisten the soil thoroughly with lukewarm water. Place in a warm, shaded place where the temperature will not fluctuate. Wait to water again for about two weeks or until you see active growth.

3 When the bud begins to grow, move the plant to a lighter area, out of direct sunlight. Water regularly to keep the soil moist but not soggy.

4 Limit water when the amaryllis is in bloom. Cool temperatures will extend the life of the blooms.

5 Continue to water as needed and fertilize every two to three weeks. The plant can be moved outdoors in spring, if desired. Bring it in and stop watering by August 1. Place it in a cool, dark place for three months. Begin the cycle again on Halloween.

How to Grow Paperwhite Narcissus

1 Place a shallow layer of activated charcoal in the bottom of the container; this will keep the water fresh. Cover the charcoal with clean gravel, stones, or marbles. Nestle the bulbs into the pot, leaving only the top half exposed. Space bulbs closely, without touching each other or the sides of the container.

2 Add water to just below the bottom of the bulbs. Place the container in the refrigerator for one week to give them a little rooting time before growing.

3 Place the container in a well lit area, away from direct sunlight. Keep the water level just below the bulbs. Place in a cool (60° to 65°F [15° to 18°C]) place at night, if possible, to keep the growth from getting too tall and weak. Bulbs will bloom in three to four weeks. Dispose of the bulbs when the blooms are spent.

You will need:

- Several paper white bulbs (as many as will fit the container without crowding)
- Watertight container, slightly deeper than the height of the bulbs
- Gravel, stones, or marbles
- Activated charcoal
- Water

Sharing Heirloom Plants

Grandmother's Christmas cactus magically blooms every December on cue. Childhood memories like these add to the mystical aura of the season. And, it is as if even the plants know when to celebrate!

Christmas cacti are triggered to bloom by a combination of cool temperatures and short days. This seems to happen naturally in the fall but can be exaggerated indoors by placing the plant in a cool dark corner 12 to 14 hours each night in late October and early November.

Heirloom plants are often passed down to someone in a succeeding generation. Unfortunately, that usually means that only one person is entrusted with the growing secrets and the responsibility to keep the plant thriving. And only that one person gets to enjoy this constant reminder of the loved one who once nurtured the plant. Luckily a Christmas cactus is one of those plants that can be easily propagated, so you can give everyone in the family their own little descendant cactus as a thoughtful Christmas gift.

The process should be started early in the year, so be sure to plan ahead. Try to take enough cuttings from the large plant so that each new plant you start will have at least three shoots.

You will need:

♦ Christmas cactus
♦ Scissors
♦ Rooting hormone
♦ High-quality potting soil
♦ 3" to 4" pots (7.5 to 10 cm)

How to Propagate a Christmas Cactus

1 After the cactus has finished blooming, snip off pieces two to three segments long, cutting at the joint between segments. Dip the cut ends into rooting hormone and leave the pieces on the work surface for several days to callous over.

2 Fill small pots with high-quality potting soil. Gently press the cut ends about ½" (1.3 cm) deep into the soil, three pieces to a pot. Place the pots in bright, indirect light, water lightly, and continue to keep the soil evenly moist. Cuttings will take about four weeks to root.

3 After two months, fertilize the cacti monthly with a balanced, water-soluble fertilizer. Stop fertilizing in late fall, when buds begin to form. Start again two months after blooming ends.

Wildlife Gift Tree

Remembering the birds at Christmastime is a wonderful tradition to start in young families. By decorating a small fir tree with seed-encrusted ornaments, suet bells, small bundles of wheat, and garlands of berries and dried fruit, kids learn the valuable lessons of sharing and caring for God's creatures. It's a tradition that rewards the giver with an exciting display of colorful birds and the antics of a few intruding squirrels.

Suet and seed bells, available at garden centers and bird-feed stores, can be tied to tree branches with craft ribbons. Small bundles of wheat can be tied directly to the branches as well. Small baskets filled with shelled corn provide a special treat for the squirrels, perhaps distracting them from robbing the special gifts intended for the birds.

You will need:

♦ Narrow Christmas craft ribbons
♦ Pinecones
♦ Peanut butter
♦ Birdseed
♦ Wheat stalks
♦ Apples, oranges, cranberries
♦ String; tapestry needle

How to Oven-dry Fresh Fruit

Slice apples and oranges crosswise, ¼" (6 mm) thick. Soak the apples in 1 qt. (0.9 L) of water with 2 tbsp. (25 mL) of lemon juice, to prevent discoloration; pat dry on paper towels. Arrange the slices on a baking sheet. Place them in an oven set at 200°F (95°C); use the exhaust fan to remove humidity as the fruit dries. Bake about two hours; timing varies with the fleshiness and quantity of the fruit. Remove when the fruit is leathery.

How to Make Birdseed Ornaments

Tie hangers around the ends of pinecones, using narrow craft ribbons. Roll the pinecones in a bowl of peanut butter. Then roll them in a bowl of birdseed.

How to Make a Bird Food Garland

Thread a tapestry needle onto a long string. Pierce in and out of dried fruit slices and through the centers of cranberries. Slide the pieces along the string, leaving small spaces between them. Here and there, tie the string around small seed-encrusted pinecones. Allow enough string at the ends for tying the garland to the tree.

How to Make an Orange Basket

Cut orange in half; scoop out the pulp. Punch three evenly spaced holes around the shell, ⅜" (1 cm) below the rim. Slip cord through each hole and knot the ends; tie free ends together to hang the basket. Fill baskets with suet, birdseed, or shelled corn.

**Photo Transfer
Quilted Diamond
Ornament
(page 18)**

Pattern shown
at 100%.

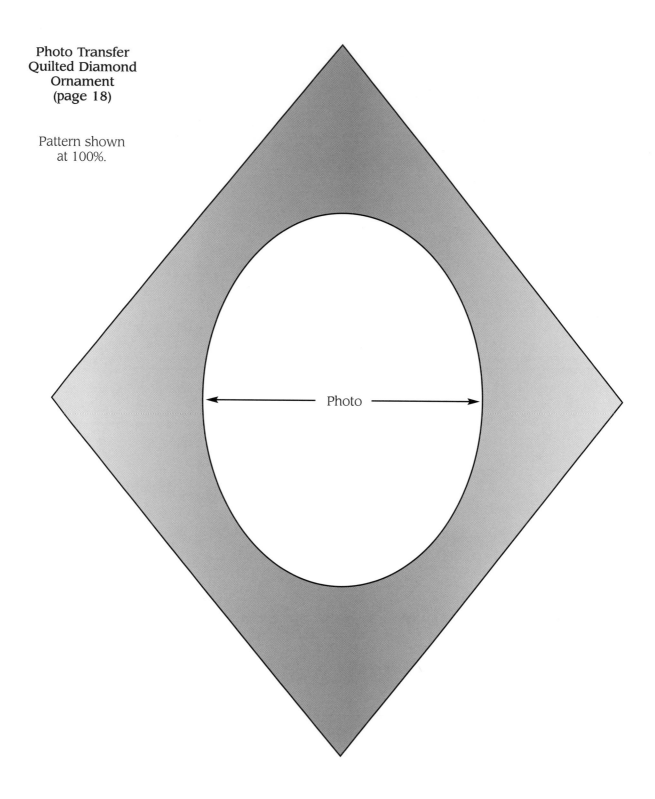

Photo

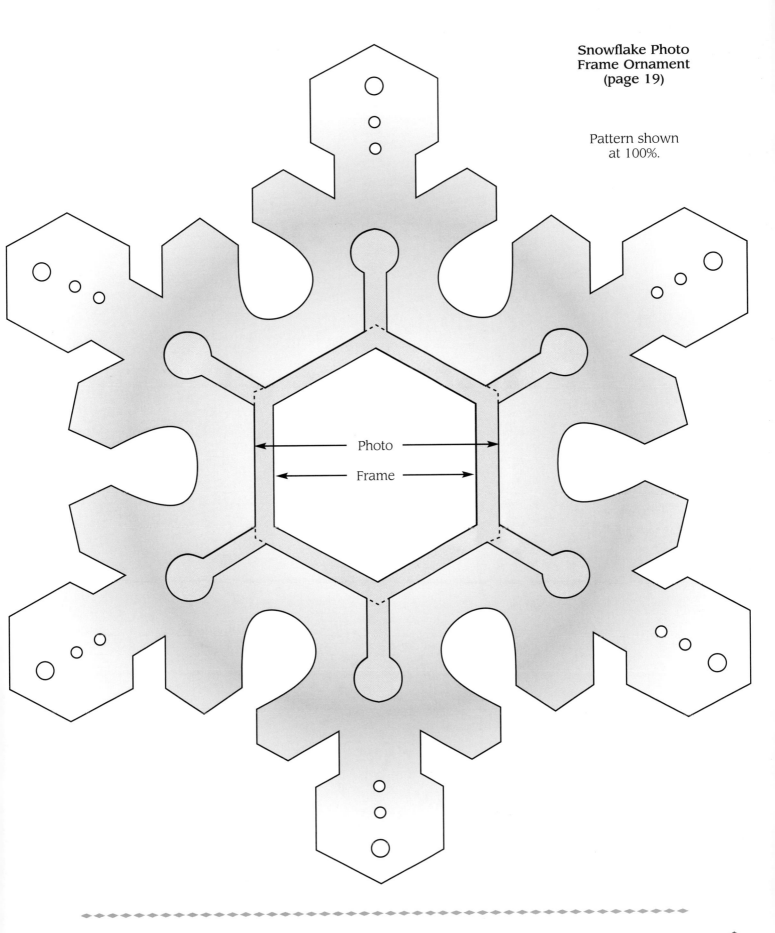

Pattern shown
at 100%.

Photo

Frame

Silk Tie
Ornaments
(pages 28 to 29)

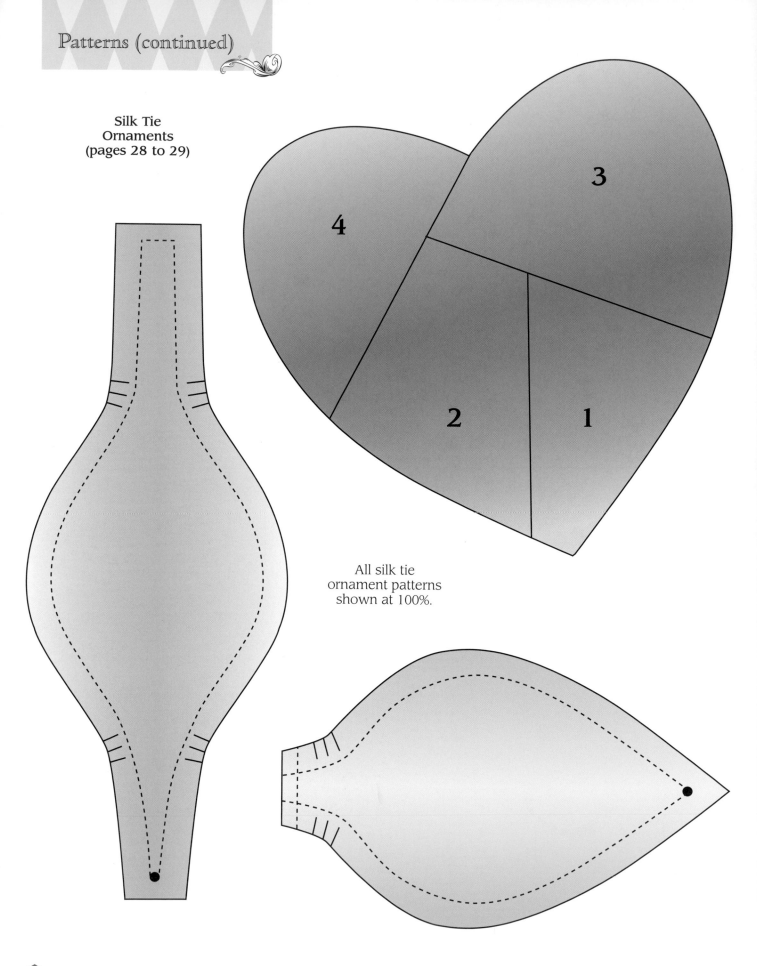

All silk tie
ornament patterns
shown at 100%.

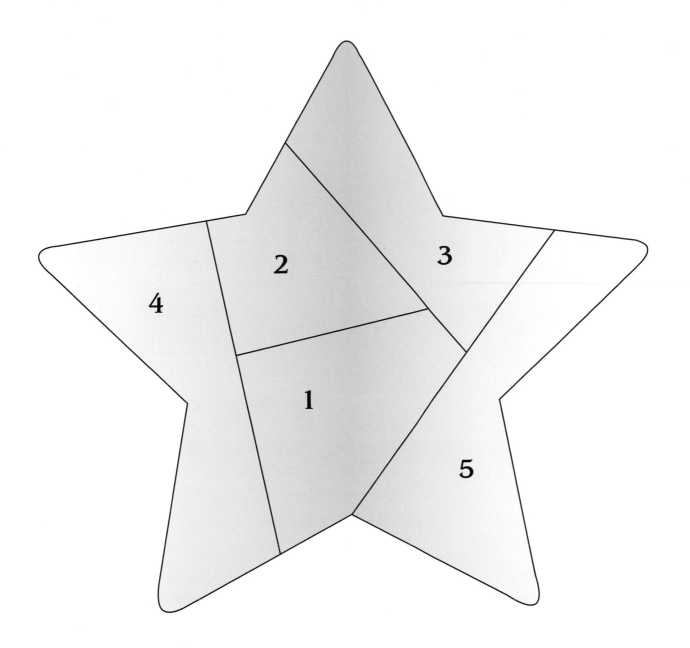

2

3

4

1

5

Christmas
Memories
Album
(page 66)

Christmas Memories

Add-a-Charm Stocking
(page 70)

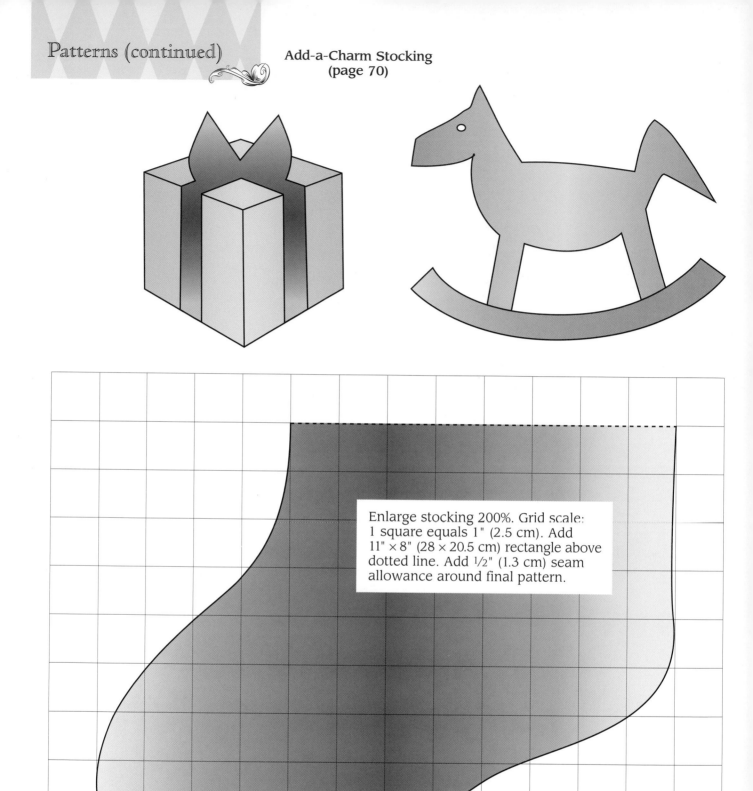

Enlarge stocking 200%. Grid scale: 1 square equals 1" (2.5 cm). Add 11" × 8" (28 × 20.5 cm) rectangle above dotted line. Add ½" (1.3 cm) seam allowance around final pattern.

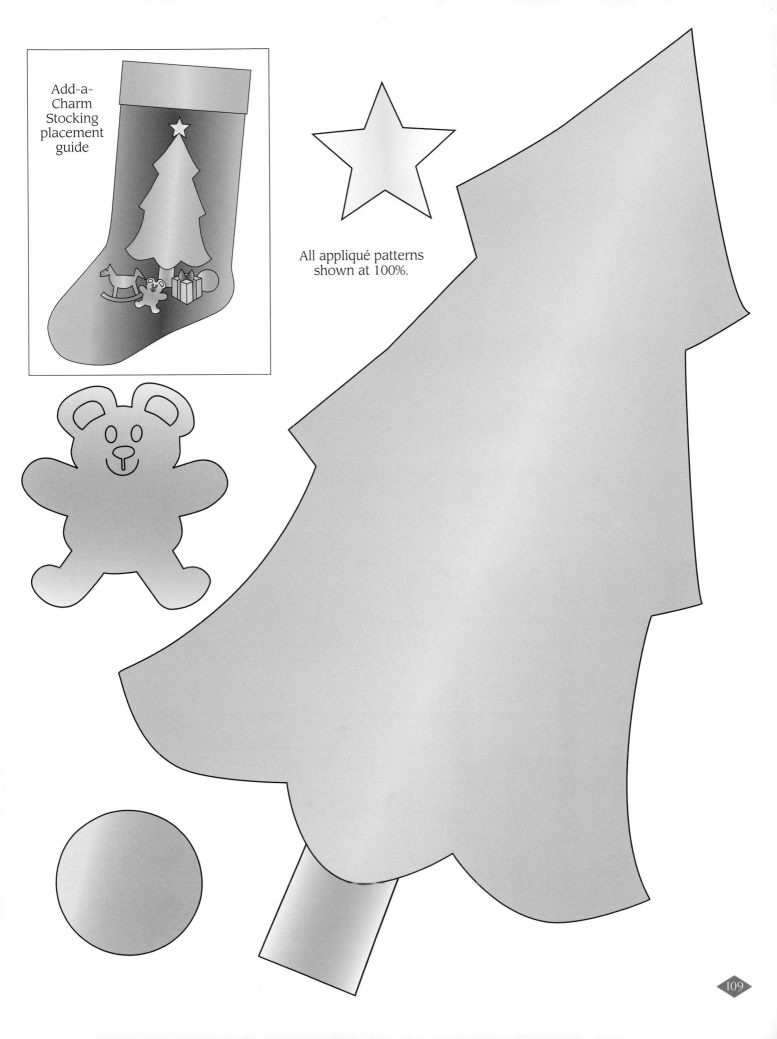

Add-a-
Charm
Stocking
placement
guide

All appliqué patterns
shown at 100%.

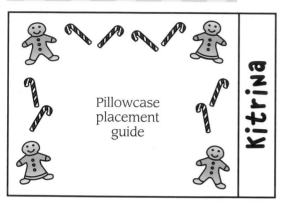

Pillowcase placement guide

Kitrina

Enlarge letters 400%.

ABCDEF
GHIJKL
MNOPQR
STUVWXYZ
abcdefg
hijklmn
opqrstu
vwxyz

Christmas Eve Pillowcase (page 72)

Appliqué patterns shown at 100%.

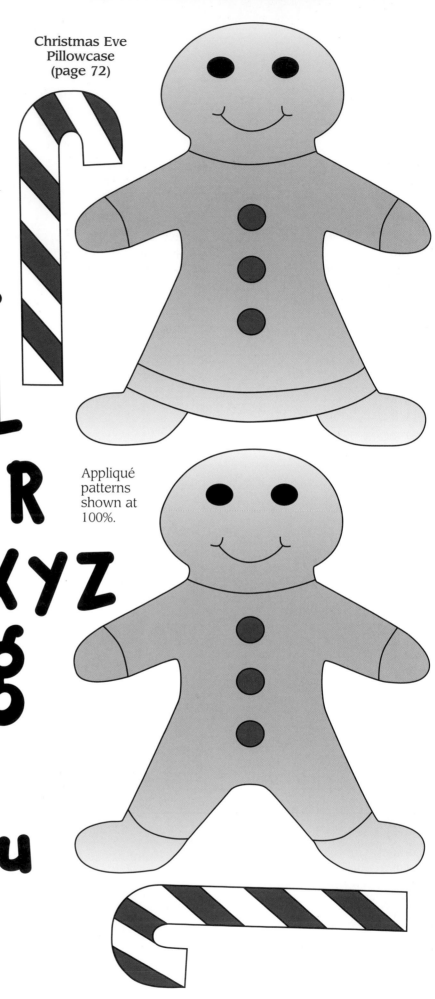

Index

A

Adhesive transfer gum (ATG) tape, 11, 61
Album,
    Christmas card, 82
    Christmas memories, 66
    Dear Santa, 90
Amaryllis bulbs, forcing blooms, 99
Angel, handkerchief, 36
Autographed Christmas tablecloth, 84–85

B

Bevel cutting mat, 12
Bird food garland, 103
Birdseed ornaments, 103
Black and white photos, tinting, 16
Bow, cluster, how to make, 46
Boxes for ornament storage, 38–40
Bulbs, forcing blooms, 98

C

Cards,
    album for, 83
    Christmas, creating, 76–81
    photo fold-out, 80
Centerpiece displays, heirloom china, 48
Chains, circle, from necktie fabric, 31
China, heirloom, in centerpiece displays, 48
Christmas cactus, preparing cuttings, 101
Coasters, photo, 15
Cookie cutter,
    ornament, 32
    tree, 33
Cookie plate for Santa, 88–89
Copper collection, 53
Countdown Christmas tree, 74
Covers, for albums, how to make, 69, 92–93
Cutouts for card making, 80

D

Decorations,
    silk tie, 28
    sleigh bells and garland, 54
Decoupage, papier-mâché ornaments, 21
Dimensional items, mounting in shadow box, 63
Dividers for storage boxes, 40
Doily ornament, crocheted, 37
Dolls, heritage, 51

E

Embossing for cards,
    pressure, 78
    thermal, 79
Exploding fold-out letter, 81

F

Fabric ball ornaments, 31
Family recipe book, 34
Feather trees, 50
Firkins, wooden, displaying, 56
Fold-out,
    card with photo, 80
    letter, 81
Folding basics for card making, 78
Frame,
    snowflake ornament, 21
    wooden, assembling, 13
Framer's tape, 61–62
Framing photos, 11
Fruit, oven dried, 103

G

Garland, bird food, 103
Gift box, to pass on, 94–97
Glass, mounting photos in, 15
Grow chart, how to make, 86–87

H

Hand tinting black and white photos, 16
Handkerchief angel, 36
Heat embossing, for cards, 79
Heirlooms in holiday displays, 45–51

Heritage dolls, 51
Horses, toy, display, 46

I

Inkjet fabric sheets, 20

J

Journal, for recording ornaments, 38, 41

L

Lace ornament with photo, 20
Letters,
    exploding fold-out, 81
    to Santa album, 90–93

M

Matting and framing photos, 11
Mounting,
    dimensional items, 63
    photo with mat, 12
    unframed photos, 63
Musical displays, 49

N

Neckties, decorations made from, 29

O

Orange basket, for birds, 103
Ornaments,
    birdseed, 103
    circle chains, 31
    cookie cutter, 32
    crocheted doily, 37
    decoupage papier-mâché, 21
    fabric ball, 31
    journal for recording history, 38, 41
    lace with photo, 20
    patchwork, 30
    photo, 19
    quilted with photo transfer, 20
    shadow box, 22
    silk tie, 28
    snowflake frame, 21
    storing, 38
    vintage, 50

Index (continued)

P

Paper frames, for mounting
  photos, 68
Paperwhite narcissus, forcing
  blooms, 99
Papier-mâché, decoupage
  ornaments, 21
Pass-it-on gift box, 94–97
Patchwork ornaments, 30
Photo,
  Christmas memories
    album, 66
  coasters, 15
  displays, 14
  fold-out cards, 80
  matting and framing, 11
  mounting in album, 68; in
    glass, 15; in shadow box, 63
  ornaments, 19
  quilt, 24–27
  Santa album, 90–93
  tinting, 16
  transfer, for quilted
    diamond, 20
  transferring to fabric, 24
Pillowcase, Christmas Eve, 72
Plant propagation, 100
Plate, Santa cookie, 88–89
Polypropylene pages for
  albums, 68

Pomanders, how to make, 52
Postcards, creating, 58–59
Pressure embossing for
  cards, 78

Q

Quilt, photo, 24–27
Quilted diamond ornament with
  photo transfer, 20

R

Recipe and cookie cutter
  ornament, 32
Recipe book, family, 34
Rubber stamps for cards, 79

S

Santa album, 90–93
Shadow box,
  display, 61
  ornaments, 22
Silk tie decorations, 28
Sleigh bells and garland
  display, 54
Snowflake frame ornament, 21
Stamped designs for cards, 79
Stenciling, for cards, 79
Stocking, Christmas
  add-a-charm, 70
Storage boxes for ornaments, 38

T

Tablecloth, autographed, 84–85
Tape,
  adhesive transfer gum (ATG)
    tape, 11
  linen framer's, 11
Thermal embossing, for
  cards, 79
Tray, heirloom, how to make,
  42–43
Tree,
  cookie cutter, 33
  wildlife gift, 102
  with countdown gifts, 74

V

Vintage ornaments, 50

W

Wildlife gift tree, 102
Woodburning, on Christmas
  tray, 43
Wooden firkins, displaying, 56
Woven ribbon greeting cards, 81
Wreath, berry, how to make, 56

Sources

Archiver's Stores
www.archiversonline.com
(albums, photo memory
supplies, papers)

C. Jenkins Necktie & Chemical Co.
39 S. Schlueter Avenue
Dellwood, MO 63135
neckties@il.net
314-521-7544
(Bubble Jet Set 2000® and
Bubble Jet Rinse®)

June Tailor
P. O. Box 208
2861 Highway 175
Richfield, WI 53076
800-844-5400
www.junetailor.com
(computer printer fabrics)

Walnut Hollow
1409 State Road 23
Dodgeville, WI 53533
www.walnuthollow.com
800-950-5101
(wooden album cover,
woodburning kits, oil color pencils,
wooden trays, wooden boxes)